GLENN

Stories of Christmas

2ND EDITION

© 2022 Glenn J. Rawson, Jean Tonioli, and Jason Tonioli

Thank you to everyone at the Glenn Rawson Stories team that helped make this book possible: Jean, Kristen, Dianna, Julie, and Sara. We would also like to thank the team at Seagull Printing for their superior printing quality. Without the help of these amazing people, we would not be able to share inspirational stories in this capacity.

All Rights Reserved. No part of this book may be reproduced in any form or by any means without permission from the authors. Requests for permission may be made by contacting the authors at GlennRawsonStories.com. The views expressed herein are the responsibility of the authors.

ISBN 979-8-8852-6326-9

Printed in the United States of America

FREE WEEKLY STORIES DELIVERED TO YOUR INBOX

SUBSCRIBE AT

GLENNRAWSONSTORIES.COM

OTHER INSPIRATIONAL TITLES BY GLENN

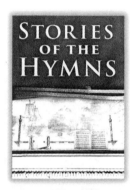

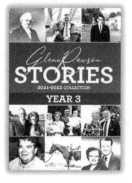

GET THESE GREAT TITLES AT
GLENNRAWSONSTORIES.COM

CUSTOMER SUBMITTED
BOOK REVIEWS

"Thank you for your stories and love of history."

- Grace C.

"Absolutely brilliant and inspiring. The stories just keep getting better."

-Ron H.

"I have enjoyed all the books I have received from you. I am especially happy with Stories of the Hymns. You were correct when you said that we wouldn't think of the songs in the same way. Thank you!

- Gloria C.

SUBSCRIBE TO GLENN'S STORIES AT
GLENNRAWSONSTORIES.COM

PROLOGUE

The Christmas season is the most anticipated and planned holiday of the year. It is a time for gathering with family, repeated traditions, singing beloved carols and songs, and service to others. We enjoy reading and sharing stories of special significance. Most importantly, it is a Christian celebration of the birth of our Savior.

This book has been written in two parts.

The first half of the book includes Christmas stories from our history, tales of the creation of favorite Christmas songs, and some personal holiday experiences which are meaningful to us.

The second part of the book is telling Christmas stories from the Bible. These are meant to be a testimony and witness of the divinity of the Lord Jesus Christ.

The telling and retelling of a story is what gives it life, and we encourage you to share these with friends and family.

Glenn Rawson, Jean Tonioli and Jason Tonioli

PART 1

Christmas is the day that holds
all time together

-Alexander Smith

Chapter One

A Holiday for the Nation

In the United States, the Christmas season is ushered in by a day to express gratitude to God. It is a national holiday——a day of Thanksgiving. It is a great time to pause and reflect on our blessings before a flurry of shopping and Christmas celebrations inundate us. Did you know this holiday would not have happened without the consistent efforts of a heroine?

In today's world, we often watch movies about superheroes. We follow stories of bold, brave, and intelligent champions. However, there are many kinds of heroes and heroines, and Thanksgiving has a pretty special one.

Sarah Josepha Buell Hale was born on October 24, 1788 in Newport, New Hampshire. As a young woman, she became a school teacher. She found that she had a talent for writing, and was the author of a poem about one of her students-- Mary Had a Little Lamb. (Yes. There really was a girl named Mary who brought a lamb to school!)

Sarah married a young lawyer named David Hale in 1813. They were very happy until David died of pneumonia when Sarah was pregnant with their fifth child. Sarah worked during the day to support her family, but at night while the children slept, she returned to her love of writing. She wrote and published her first novel, and this led to a job as editor at a new magazine for women called Boston's Ladies' Magazine and later working for Godey's Lady's Book.

Sarah was a superhero because she knew the power of the pen. Every magazine issue had an editorial written by Sarah. She supported causes which she felt were important and encouraged her readers to write letters seeking change as well.

In 1789, President George Washington issued a proclamation designating November 26 of that year as a National Day of Thanksgiving to recognize the role of providence in the creation of the new United States. Sarah loved Thanksgiving, but it was celebrated mainly in New England where she lived and other northern states. The rest of the country was ignoring this day to give thanks more and more. In her editorials, as well as writing thousands of letters to politicians, she advocated for every state, and the whole country, to celebrate a day of thanks together. One by one, individual states made a Thanksgiving holiday, although not on the same day.

Sarah believed that the nation needed to come together and give thanks on the same holiday, just like a family. So, she used her magazine platform and began petitioning the President of the United States for a national holiday.

President Zachary Taylor refused. President Millard Fillmore rejected it. Sarah persisted over the years. She petitioned President Franklin Pierce and he would not consider it. She wrote a personal letter to President James Buchanan, asking that the whole country gather together on the fourth Thursday in November. President Buchanan said that he had more important things to deal with as the country wrestled with the issue of slavery.

Discouraged as things in the country descended into a civil war, the North against the South, the 74-year-old magazine editor wrote a letter to President Lincoln on September 28, 1863, urging him to have the "day of our annual Thanksgiving made a national and fixed Union Festival." She explained that it was necessary to have "national recognition… to become permanently an American custom and institution." President Lincoln agreed. On October 3, 1863, President Abraham Lincoln issued a proclamation declaring the last Thursday of November as a day of Thanksgiving for the whole country.

Over a period of 36 years, Sarah Hale, a true superhero, used her pen and persevered, helping to bring the holiday we know of as Thanksgiving to her country. Her message to us today would be the same as President Washington and President Lincoln, imploring fellow Americans to find time in their family gatherings to count their blessings, unite as a people, and be thankful for living in the United States of America.

Source:

https://www.abrahamlincolnonline.org/lincoln/speeches/thanks.htm

Lincoln and Thanksgiving - Lincoln Home National Historic Site (U.S. National Park Service)

The Priest Of The Poor

Joseph Franz Mohr was born in Salzburg, Austria on 11 December 1792. Joseph grew up without his father – just his mother, grandmother, and a stepsister. Notwithstanding their poverty, Joseph displayed uncommon talent and intelligence and was sponsored to obtain a university education, where at the same time he sang in the choir and played the violin.

After graduation in 1811, he enrolled in the seminary to become a priest, which required special permission from the Church. Permission was granted and by 1815, he was ordained a priest at the age of 23. In that same year, he was appointed assistant priest in Mariapfarr. It was there in 1816 that he wrote these now famous words:

> *Silent Night, Holy Night!*
> *All is calm, all is bright,*
> *Round yon virgin mother and child.*
> *Holy infant so tender and mild.*
> *Sleep in heavenly peace;*
> *Sleep in heavenly peace.*

On August 25, 1817, Joseph Mohr became the assistant priest in the new parish of Oberndorf. It was there that he met and became friends with Franz Xaver Gruber, who oversaw the choir and organ at the St. Nikola Church.

Just before Christmas 1818, Joseph Mohr brought the poem he had written to Franz Gruber and asked him to compose a melody. Gruber agreed and composed a most fitting and tender melody, and together the two friends sang the song for the first time in the Church at St. Nikola following the Christmas Mass. Joseph accompanied on the guitar.

From there, Joseph Mohr went on to a life of dedicated service to the Church and his people. He became known as the "Priest of the Poor." He passed away December 4, 1848. "His only estate was his guitar." Joseph Mohr "never witnessed the success that his Christmas hymn would have throughout the world."

And just one more thing…the Christmas hymn, Silent Night is Christmas! It captures our hearts and souls and invokes the peace that was the wondrous birth of the Prince of Peace. Maybe it is altogether fitting that Joseph Mohr was given those meaningful words, for you see, Joseph Mohr's birth was considered a "crime." He was born out of wedlock, abandoned by his father, shunned by society, and stigmatized by his Church. And yet, like the Master he served, he loved and lifted the children of the poor.

Sources:

https://www.stillenacht.com/en/protagonists/joseph-mohr-1792-1848/

https://www.german-way.com/history-and-culture/holidays-and-celebrations/christmas/stille-nacht-silent-night/

Chapter Three

That Providential Failure

Phillip graduated from Harvard University at the age of 19 and accepted employment as a teacher in the Boston Latin School in September 1855. This would be the first step in his life-goal of becoming a professor. Shortly after, he wrote to a friend and said,

"Seriously, I like the life. Isn't there a sort of satisfaction and pleasure in knowing that you are doing, or at least have the chance of doing something. At Cambridge it was all very well, but we had only ourselves to work on. Here we have some twenty, thirty, or forty on whom we can bring to bear the authority and influence of a superior position and see what we can make out of them and watch all their workings."

He taught Greek, Latin, and French, and all went well for the fall semester, but then at the opening of the winter term, he was transferred to a class of older boys and things began to go awry. It would seem that his students did not like him and began to rebel. "They are the most disagreeable set of creatures without exception I ever met with." As expected, it took a terrible toll on him. "I am tired, sick, cross, and almost dead," he said.

The situation came to a head by February 1856, and Phillip was forced to resign—a failure. He is reported to have said,

"I do not know what will become of me and I do not care much…. I wish I were fifteen years old again. I believe I might become a stunning man: but somehow or other, I do not seem in the way to come to much now."

It was a depressing and dark time for Phillip. Humiliated and inconsolable, he wandered the streets of Boston. There was no one he could unburden his heart to. Did he even comprehend the burden himself? One biographer wrote of him, "The failure of Phillip Brooks on the threshold of life was conspicuous and complete, momentous also, and, it may be said in view of his later career, providential."

Phillip awoke to his heritage. He was the son of generations of famous clergymen, and now the faith of his fathers became his. Born anew, he set a course to study for the ministry. He entered the seminary and prepared to be ordained in the Episcopal Church. He graduated in 1859, and was ordained a deacon. In 1860, he was ordained a priest, and by 1869, was called to serve in Boston's Church of the Holy Trinity. One writer said this of the life legacy of Phillip Brooks:

"Brooks quickly became Boston's first citizen, knowing the sheer adulation of the worshipers who regularly packed Trinity to hear his compelling sermons and to view his serene yet radiant presence. His fame spread. In the entire annals of the Episcopal Church, the power of his preaching is unmatched." Invitation after invitation to preach came his way, as did honorary degrees from the nation's leading universities and England's Oxford. Greatly admired abroad, he was the first American to preach in the Royal Chapel at Windsor. In 1891, he was elected bishop of Massachusetts, the culmination of a life of nobility. His unexpected death in 1893, caused Lord Bryce to observe that not since Lincoln's assassination had America so widely mourned the loss of a leader.

While no one today has ever heard the voice of Phillip Brooks preaching in his powerful, humble, and charismatic way, yet all of us have heard and even sung one of Phillip Brooks greatest sermons.

At Christmastime 1865, Phillip Brooks was riding horseback from Jerusalem to Bethlehem, where he assisted with the midnight services on Christmas Eve. He would later write of that moment:

"I remember standing in the old Church in Bethlehem, close to the spot where Jesus was born, when the whole Church was ringing hour after hour with splendid hymns of praise to God, how again and again it seemed as if I could hear voices I knew well, telling each other of the wonderful night of the Savior's birth."

This sacred experience awakened in Brooks the desire to write his own hymn of praise to commemorate that holy night. Lewis Redner, a friend of Brooks said,

"As Christmas of 1868 approached, Mr. Brooks told me that he had written a simple little carol for the Christmas Sunday-school service, and he asked me to write the tune to it. The simple music was written in great haste and under great pressure. We were to practice on the following Sunday. Mr. Brooks came to me on Friday, and said, "Redner, have you ground out that music yet....'?" I replied, "No", but that he should have it by Sunday. On the Saturday night before, my brain was all confused about the tune. I thought more about my Sunday-school lesson than I did about the music. But I was roused from sleep late in the night, hearing an angel-strain whispering in my ear, and seizing a piece of music paper, I jotted down the treble of the tune as we now have it, and on Sunday morning before going to church, I filled in the harmony. Neither Mr. Brooks nor I ever thought the carol or the music to it would live beyond that Christmas of 1868."

That enduring Christmas Carol—that lasting and most famous sermon by Reverend Phillip Brooks...O Little Town of Bethlehem.

Oh little town of Bethlehem, how still we see thee lie

Above thy deep and dreamless sleep the silent stars go by

Yet in thy dark streets shineth, the everlasting light

The hopes and fears of all the years are met in thee tonight.

For Christ is born of Mary, and gathered all above

While mortals sleep the angels keep their watch of wondering love

Oh morning stars together, proclaim thy holy birth.

And praises sing to God the king, and peace to men on earth.

Oh little town of Bethlehem, how still we see thee lie

Above thy deep and dreamless sleep the silent stars go by

Yet in thy dark streets shineth, the everlasting light

The hopes and fears of all the years are met in thee tonight.

Sources:

https://archive.org/details/phillipsbroo1800alle/page/18/mode/2up https://archive.org/details/phillipsbroo1800alle/page/20/mode/2up

https://en.wikipedia.org/wiki/Phillips_Brooks

https://archive.org/details/phillipsbroo1800alle/page/20/mode/2up

https://biography.yourdictionary.com/phillips-brooks

https://en.wikipedia.org/wiki/O_Little_Town_of_Bethlehem

Chapter Four

The Banned Celebration

We all know about the Pilgrims, a group of Puritan Separatists who came to America for religious freedom and celebrated the well-known First Thanksgiving in 1621. However, when it came to observing Christmas, it was on the chopping block.

European Christmas traditions of the time included loud caroling, public drinking, feasting, and boisterous behavior. The Puritans wanted nothing to do with such celebrations or the Catholic and Anglican churches, which they had left Europe for the New World to avoid. They scorned Christian religious holidays like Christmas and Easter because they were not mentioned in the Bible and the date of Christ's birth was not listed. Furthermore, the Puritans regarded Christmas as a remnant of paganism. They considered fourth-century Christians as acting blasphemously, borrowing December 25th from a pagan festival, Saturnalia, which celebrated the winter solstice. They wanted to abandon any traditions that they thought interfered with the sanctity of Christianity. The devout Puritans were having none of it!

Reverend John Robinson, a Pilgrim spiritual leader, lamented that individuals who celebrated Easter and Christmas were NOT true Christians as long as they persisted in recognizing these days. A woman named Increase Mather wrote in her diary that "men dishonor Christ more in the 12 days of Christmas than in all 12 months of the year."

The Pilgrims first arrived on the Mayflower on December 21, 1620. On Christmas Day, men left the ship to cut and saw timber to build houses. Passengers who stayed on the ship did enjoy some beer from the ship's provisions, but that was the extent of the merrymaking.

Almost a year later, in November 1621, a second group of colonists arrived in Plymouth. They were mostly bachelors, and unlike the original colonists, they did not come for only religious reasons. They were seeking financial gain from the abundant land and resources of the area.

The Pilgrims got ready to go to work on Christmas morning, 1621. However, some of the newcomers to the colony objected. Governor Bradford wrote that "most of the new company excused themselves and said it went against their consciences to work on that day." Since it was a matter of conscience, Bradford agreed to "spare them until they were better informed." The governor assumed that they would return to their homes and privately celebrate Christmas in prayer. On returning from work, Governor Bradford was appalled to find the men openly playing sports such as pitching the barr and stoole-ball [similar to cricket] in the street. Bradford confiscated their sports equipment, saying "there should be no gaming or reveling in the streets" and it was "against his conscience that they should play and others work."

Apparently, not every person living in the colony rejected Christmas. Because some people still made merry, a law was deemed necessary. In 1659, the law book of the Massachusetts Bay Colony shows an edict banning Christmas. It said that to prevent disorders arising in several places, by observing such festivals "that were superstitiously kept in other countries," that anyone who was found "observing any such day as Christmas or the like, either by forbearing of labor [not working], feasting, or any other way" would pay a fine of five shillings to the county. Laws suppressing celebrating Christmas were repealed in 1681, but Puritan believers refused to condone it. Evergreen decorations, associated with paganism, were forbidden in Puritan meeting houses and discouraged in individual homes. Merrymakers were still prosecuted for disturbing the peace.

In 1856, Christmas became a public holiday in Massachusetts and was declared a National holiday in 1870. However, that same year, classes were scheduled in Boston public schools on Christmas Day—and punishments were given out to children who chose to stay home and with their families to celebrate!

If we judge the Puritan settlers through the lens of 21st century standards, we would condemn their lack of tolerance. However, it is good to remember that their motive for coming to America was for religious freedom as Christians, to worship God as they believed was correct. Each man and woman have the right to choose how, when, and if they worship, thanks to the sacrifices of many people. We honor their legacy that helped shape our country.

Sources:

https://www.theatlantic.com/ideas/archive/2021/11/how-lincoln-redefined-thanksgiving-and-christmas/620800/

https://newengland.com/today/living/new-england-history/how-the-puritans-banned-christmas/

https://www.boston.com/news/history/2017/12/25/plymouth-colony-christmas-1621/

Chapter Five

Hallelujah

One of our most treasured musical traditions at Christmas had its beginning in a city in central Germany, with a child who disobeyed his father's wishes.

Georg was born on a winter day in February 1685, welcomed by his parents Dorothea and Georg, and five siblings from his father's first marriage. The family lived in Halle, Germany, where his father had a prominent position serving a local duke as a barber-surgeon. Young Georg's father wanted him to become a lawyer. However, from an early age, Georg longed to study music. His father objected, doubting that the pursuit of music would be a good source of income. Because of his father's definite opinion, the boy was not permitted to even own a musical instrument or take part in any musical pursuit.

This did not deter the determined youngster or his supportive mother. Unknown to his father, the child was given a small clavichord which was stealthily placed in the tiny, top room of the house. While the rest of the family slept at night, Georg would creep into the room and quietly play the instrument. When he was eight years old, he surprised his family and friends at the end of a church meeting, when he climbed onto the organ bench and began to play a song. The listeners had no idea that he was so talented. Yet, his father stood firm as he reminded his son that he needed a career more practical than music.

When he was barely eleven, the Duke of Weissenfels heard Georg play the organ, and recognizing the boy's genius, helped persuade his father to allow his son to study music.

Georg excelled in his classes, learning the principles of keyboard performance and composition.

Sadly, Georg's father died shortly before his twelfth birthday, but his education was still provided for. The 12-year-old youth continued his music studies and later he accepted a position as a church organist. In an effort to honor his late father, Georg enrolled as a law student at the University of Halle. However, before his legal training was completed, the allure of a musical career led him to Hamburg, where greater musical opportunities were available. He played several instruments in an orchestra and began to compose music.

We know this child prodigy today as the composer Georg Frederic Handel. By the age of eighteen, he had written his first opera. After working as a musician and composer for several royal courts in Europe, he moved to England, where he lived for most of his life.

As the popularity of Italian operas which he had been writing began to decrease, Handel turned his attention to writing oratorios. In July of 1741, he received the text for an oratorio from Charles Jennens, with the understanding that it would be performed for Easter the following year. Jennens wrote to a friend that he hoped Handel would lay out his whole genius and skill to make it his best composition yet.

Jennens' text was a narrative called Messiah, and written in three parts: the first prophesied the birth of Jesus Christ; the second told of the Savior's sacrifice for humankind, and the final section heralded the Lord's resurrection. During 24 days in August and September of 1741, Handel set to work and poured his soul into composing the 259-page oratorio. It is estimated that there were about a quarter of a million notes in the music, with very few errors in the initial manuscript notes. Working for ten hours a day, that means he was writing 15 notes a minute! It was said that he locked himself in a room and began writing in a burst of inspiration, going for long periods without food or sleep.

It is clear that Handel himself knew the work was his best, and that the Hallelujah chorus was exceptional. After completing the work, the story goes that he exclaimed, "I did think I saw heaven open, and saw the very face of God." At the end of his manuscript, Handel wrote the letters "SDG"— Soli Deo Gloria — "To God alone the glory".

The Messiah was first performed in the Musick Hall in Dublin on April 13, 1742. Seven hundred people attended the premiere. The ladies were asked to not wear their hooped skirts to make more seating in the room. The Dublin News-Letter described the oratorio as "... far surpassing anything of that nature which has been performed in this or any other kingdom." Handel donated the proceeds of one of the concerts to three charities, including 142 people who had their debts paid and were released from debtor's prison.

In March of 1743, the Messiah premiered in London, with equally positive reviews. It became the custom for audiences to stand for the "Hallelujah" chorus. One story claimed that King George II was in attendance and was so moved by the music that he stood up – and if the king stood, then everyone else in the room was obliged to stand as well. There is no fact checker to prove if the king attended one of the performances or not, but there is documentation that many audience members were so moved that they spontaneously stood. Whether royal example, religious devotion, repeated ritual, or wonderful musicality is the cause, audiences continue to stand during this song today.

In the United States, the first documented performance of selections from the Messiah was done in December 1815 in Boston by the Handel and Haydn Society. On Christmas Day in 1818, the society gave the American premiere of Handel's

Messiah in full, and a new holiday tradition was born. In the late 19th century, performances of the Messiah became an even stronger yuletide tradition in the United States than in Britain.

The Messiah, the world's most famous musical oratorio, is performed every holiday season by hundreds, if not thousands, of amateur and professional groups around the world. It is no wonder that audiences are moved to stand in worshipful praise as they hear the chorus of Hallelujah! For the Lord God omnipotent reigneth. And He shall reign forever and ever. King of Kings and Lord of Lords. Hallelujah!

Sources:

https://91classical.org/post/how-handels-messiah-became-an-american-christmas-tradition/

https://www.smithsonianmag.com/arts-culture/the-glorious-history-of-handels-messiah-148168540/

https://www.bsomusic.org/stories/5-things-you-might-not-know-about-handels-messiah/

https://www.thetabernaclechoir.org/messiah/george-frideric-handel-a-brief-history.html

Chapter Six

Creating Christmas

The year was 1824. A twelve-year-old boy named Charles lived with his parents, John and Elizabeth, and six siblings, in a poor neighborhood in Camden, a district of northwest London, England. His father worked as a pay clerk in the Royal Navy, receiving an income which required strict and careful money management to support his household. Before moving to Camden, his family had spent five years living in Chatham. Charles had loved those happy, carefree years. As a young boy there, his mother had taught him how to read. He even attended school in Chatham for two years, although much of his early education came from the things he read. By the time Charles was ten, he had devoured challenging books like Robinson Crusoe and Don Quixote, and even written a play.

When his father John's work posting changed to London, Charles became aware of a serious family problem. His parents had the habit of spending more money each month than his father earned, and John was in debt to many creditors. In fact, he owed more money than he could earn in multiple years. The family had moved into cheaper, crowded quarters and bill collectors often knocked on their door. A baker, James Kerr, one of many people who John owed money to, insisted he be paid the £40 and 10-shillings which were due. In an attempt to pay the debt, all of the family's household goods, including furniture and silverware, were sold. Unfortunately, that didn't raise enough money.

Charles' father was sent to Marshalsea Debtor's Prison, a place where people who could not repay their bills were imprisoned. His wife and younger children would later live there with him in shared rooms. Charles' parents decided that their bookish second child needed to leave school and help support them. A room was found for Charles to sleep in, and the twelve-year-old boy took a job for six shillings a week at Warren's Blacking Factory. It was a rundown business which was owned by one of his mother's relatives. The building on the banks of the River Thames was filthy, and had rotting boards in the floors and staircase. Rats swarmed in the cellars and boldly came up the stairs by the workers. Charles was ridiculed and harassed by the older boys who worked there, intellectually frustrated, and resentful. For ten hours a day, six days a week, he stood by a window for better light, filling and tying off small pots with shoe blacking [polish], and pasting labels on the containers.

Looking back on that time years later, Charles saw it was then that he lost his youthful innocence, saying that he questioned "how [he] could be so easily cast away at such a young age." Though he visited his family at the prison weekly, he cried often and felt abandoned. John was released from Marshalsea Prison three months later, after paying his debts with money he inherited from his mother's will.

The family's financial situation was still tenuous, and Charles' mother, Elizabeth, insisted that he remain working at the factory to provide income for the family. His father agreed. Charles was devastated. He wished for a life where he could continue studying and learning, escaping the poverty which surrounded him. Adding insult to injury, one day he looked out the factory window and saw his own father, now a free man, in a crowd gawking at him. After many more months, John's father had employment and young Charles was able to leave the factory and briefly return to school. At fifteen, family problems and lack of money required him to stop any formal education and go to work.

As an adult, Charles told a friend," I know how all these things have worked together to make me what I am, but

I never afterwards forgot, I never shall forget, I never can forget." Over the next seven years, while helping to support his family, he worked as an office boy, a law clerk, and reporter. Thirsting for knowledge, he continued his education. He bought a reading ticket to the British Museum and voraciously read many of the books in that large library. He even taught himself shorthand, a skill which was an advantage as a clerk and reporter. Who was this young man who found success in spite of so many obstacles? We know him today as Charles John Huffam Dickens – one of the most accomplished writers in the English language. He published twenty novels in his lifetime and all of them are still in print today.

The painful experiences of his youth, poverty, and social injustice were often the subjects of his writing. His stories, which were published in magazines a chapter at a time, became extremely popular. By 1837, when the installments were put in book form, Charles Dickens quickly became the most popular author of the day. In the following years, additional novels were written and well received, but Charles knew that his financial stability always depended upon the popularity of the next book which he would write.

In the fall of 1843, Charles was in desperate need of money. His current serialized novel was not selling as well as the previous ones had, and his publishers wanted to decrease his income from £200 to £150 per month – which would have been extremely difficult. Charles was a married man with four children and a fifth on the way, and as happened far too often throughout his life, his father needed extra money due to his extravagance and poor money management. Charles needed to write a book quickly.

That fall, Charles had visited schools for the poor in the slums, called "ragged schools" because of the worn clothes of children who came to them. He encountered children who lived as thieves and pickpockets to survive, just as he had seen in his own days of poverty. Charles was a champion of the poor and felt that Victorian society needed to treat its poorest and neediest members better. He hated child labor, hunger, and neglect. When half of the recorded deaths in London at that time were children, how could society turn a blind eye? He wondered how he could convey the urgency and "strike a sledge blow" for the poor.

Later that month, after attending meetings where he was a speaker in support of education in Manchester, England, a center of industrialization and child labor, Charles strode alone in the darkened streets of the city. His companions were the ghosts of his past and the images of those living in poverty who he had recently seen. They coalesced into characters for a new tale – a story about Christmas. His nightly walks continued when he returned to London, his mind whirling. As the tale unfolded, he wept and laughed as the characters came to life. He became completely absorbed in the story, even canceling appointments or meetings with friends.

At that time in Britain, the celebration of Christmas had declined and it was considered a minor holiday. That was about to change. In the opening pages of Dickens' tale, the adult nephew of the miserly main character, Ebenezer Scrooge, said, "A Merry Christmas, uncle! God save you!" Fred also said, "But I am sure I have always thought of Christmas time…apart from…its sacred name and origin… as a good time, a kind, forgiving, charitable, pleasant time… when men and women…open up their shut-up hearts freely, and to think of people below them as if they were fellow-passengers to the grave, and not another race of creatures bound on other journeys." The holiday "has done me good… and will do me good; and I say, God bless it."

Charles created an image of a Merry Christmas, full of joy, empathy, and family togetherness, which has become a blueprint for many of our holiday celebrations. However, he needed something more, a type of fairy tale or fantasy, to hold the interest of his audience. Through a ghost story, with Scrooge's friend Marley, and the ghosts of Christmas Past, Present, and Future, he was able to convey the need for compassion and charity to those less fortunate. The miserable miser, Scrooge, turned into a soul of generosity and goodwill. In the story, Scrooge opened his eyes to the needs of the less fortunate, and was determined to improve the lives of his clerk's family and others in his sphere of influence. He also witnessed many of the things which we hold dear today in our Christmas celebrations: gathering with family, plenteous food and drink, turkeys, plum pudding, presents, games, caroling, and giving money to help those less fortunate. Future readers of the story enthusiastically embraced the activities from the story, which became treasured traditions.

A Christmas Carol is often called Charles Dickens' best story – a short tale of fewer than 30,000 words and conceived and written in less than six weeks. Upon completion of the tale, he wrote to a friend, saying, "I believe I have written a tremendous book; and knocked the Carol out of the field. It will make a great uproar, I have no doubt."

Because his publishers were not keen on spending extra money on the tale, Charles personally oversaw the publishing details. He did not initially make as much money on the book due to the costs incurred. A Christmas Carol was first published on December 19, 1843, with the 6,000 first edition copies sold out by Christmas Eve, and by 1844, it had gone through 13 printings.

More than 175 years later, this story, written by a self-educated writer who wanted to bring awareness and opportunity to the less fortunate, still inspires countless people every Christmas season. Through the character of Scrooge, Charles Dickens encouraged his readers to keep

Christmas when he said, "I will honour Christmas in my heart, and try to keep it all the year." May we look beyond ourselves and help those in need, as Scrooge resolved to do, and remember Tiny Tim's simple blessing for us all as he exclaimed, "God bless us, everyone!"

Sources:

Standiford, L. (2008). The Man Who Invented Christmas. Broadway Books, New York.

https://en.wikipedia.org/wiki/John_Dickens

https://www.biography.com/news/charles-dickens-a-christmas-carol

https://www.cliffsnotes.com/literature/g/great-expectations/harles-dickens-biography

Dickens, C. (1980). A Christmas Carol. Watermill Press, New York.

https://www.arts.gov/stories/blog/2020/ten-things-know-about-charles-dickens-christmas-carol

https://www.charlesdickenspage.com

Chapter Seven

The Christmas Gift of Freedom

Does God care about human freedom? Can a man be saved in bondage? Now, these are important questions. By way of an answer, I have an unusual Christmas story I would like to share with you.

It was December 1776. The tattered remnants of George Washington's Continental Army were camped in the open on the banks of the Delaware River. Where once they had been some 20,000 in number, bold and strong, now they were less than 6,000. Where once they had soundly defeated the British at Lexington and Concord, now they were a decimated band running for their lives across the frozen New Jersey landscape, with the British in hot, humiliating pursuit.

And now here they were, huddled around fires to keep from freezing, their rations reduced to starvation subsistence, even living on tree bark. Their inadequate clothing was nothing more than filthy rags hanging on emaciated bodies. They were dejected and defeated, as beaten psychologically as they were physically. Yet, on this ragtag group of men hung all the hopes of the American Revolution. This was the army. They were all that stood between America and avowed British tyranny.

Consider, if you will, General Washington. At this time, he was about as burdened a man as ever lived. Many were calling for his resignation, even within the Continental Congress. Officers within his own command were openly murmuring against him, and positioning to replace him. Desertion[s] within the ranks of his army were rampant and daily. Here he stood on the banks of the Delaware, with an army seemingly too weak to fight, feeling the weight, and carrying the blame of the American plight.

Meanwhile, across the river in Trenton, safe and warm, were the Hessian mercenaries, left by General Howe to hold Washington's pitiful army at bay. He could have finished them at any time, but it was widely known that on December 31st, the enlistments of Washington's army expired. The men would go home. The British saw no need to attack and finish them off. Cold, starvation, desertion—they would finish the fight for them. All the British and the Germans needed to do was sit and watch while the American Revolution collapsed upon itself, and the dream, that arrogant dream of American freedom, to die with it. I don't need to tell you, this was a monumental historical moment.

At one of the lowest points, Thomas Paine came into camp, talking and mingling with the soldiers. He was deeply moved by their plight, sat down, and according to some, penned a pamphlet called "The American Crisis" on the head of a drum. These are some of those words he wrote at that critical time:

"These are the times that try men's souls: the summer soldier and the sunshine patriot will, in this crisis, shrink from the service of his country, but he that stands it now, deserves the love and thanks of man and woman. Tyranny, like hell, is not easily conquered, yet we have this consolation with us, that the harder the conflict, the more glorious the triumph. What we obtain too cheap, we esteem too lightly: it is dearness only that gives everything its value. Heaven knows how to put a proper price upon its goods; and it would be strange indeed, if so celestial an article as Freedom should not be highly rated" (The American Crisis I, December 19, 1776).

These words caused a storm through America. To the credit of the man and the power of heaven that moved him, Washington was inspired by these words, and by the powers of Heaven. He did not lie down in defeat. He rose from his knees, gathered his ragged and beaten army, and in the face of a terrible howling blizzard, crossed the Delaware on Christmas night, 1776. Several thousand men, cannon, and horses were ferried across the ice-choked, black waters of the Delaware. From there, Washington marched his men nine miles to Trenton, leaving bloody footprints in the snow as he went—in weather literally so cold that men froze to death the moment they sat down. At dawn, Washington did the impossible with the incapable. He attacked Trenton and the unsuspecting Hessians, and captured the men and the city—and lost not a single man in the battle.

Inspired by that timely victory, the faltering fight for American freedom regained its momentum. Men reenlisted, volunteers came, allies joined, and the battle for freedom went on to victory. Washington, over the next few days, captured Princeton and sufficient supplies to carry his men through the winter, safely quartered at Morristown.

But oh, think about that moment when it would have been so easy to give up the fight and quit. Thank God for that man. Thank God for those men! Little did they know how much their sacrifice would change the course of human history, and change our lives. I tell you, with all of my soul, the cause of freedom is the cause of Christ. His birth signaled the opening of the prison doors. No man can be saved in bondage, political or spiritual. We must be free in heart and in person.

Praise be to God for an oft-forgotten Christmas gift, given by humble men and women at great cost. Thanks be to God and Merry Christmas!

Chapter Eight

Joy

One of the best loved Christmas carols we sing today includes contributions from three gifted individuals who never met, and was not even written to be a song about the sacred circumstances surrounding the birth of Jesus.

The man who wrote the text for the song was considered a nonconformist and a bit of a rebel by many in his country. Isaac Watts (1674-1748) was born in Southampton, England to parents who were dissenters from the Church of England. At an early age, Isaac showed a gift for rhyming and writing. He grew up in a world where music in every church meeting consisted of only psalms from the Old Testament, or scriptures put to music. As a young man, Watts complained to his father of the monotonous hymn singing, which people in the congregation did poorly and without feeling. His father challenged him to write something better, and that is exactly what he did.

Every week for two years, Isaac wrote a new text for a song. He paraphrased most of the Psalms and also included some of his personal interpretations of the scriptures. These updated texts were well received by church members, but critics described his writing as "worldly" and inappropriate. His work was published, and in the collection of 210 Hymns and Spiritual Songs he explained:

"While we sing the praises of God in His church, we are employed in that part of worship which of all others is the nearest akin to heaven, and 'tis pity that this of all others should be performed the worst upon earth."

Writing hundreds of hymn texts in his lifetime, Isaac Watts is recognized today as the "Godfather of English Hymnody." One of the hymns that he wrote, which was published in 1719, was based on parts of Psalm 98. Verse four states, "Make a joyful noise unto the Lord, all the earth: make a loud noise, and rejoice, and sing praise." The song celebrated Christ's second coming to the earth.

The second collaborator was Georg Friederic Handel (1685-1759), the popular German-born composer who lived in London. Isaac Watts and Handel were contemporaries in England, but did not collaborate on this hymn. Handel's most famous work today is the Messiah. His part was acknowledged by the third contributor to the carol.

Across the Atlantic in the United States, and more than a century later, an American music director and educator, who became known as the "Father of American Church Music", Lowell Mason (1792-1872), was writing music and producing books of hymns. His tunes were often influenced by the work of European classical composers, including Georg Friederic Handel. While living in Boston, he served as president of Handel and Haydn Society and worked as music superintendent for the Boston school system. He was a champion of youth music education and is even credited today with writing the tune for the children's nursery rhyme Mary Had a Little Lamb. One of the musical styles which Lowell Mason used in his melodies was "fuging", where voice parts entered one after the other in rapid succession, usually repeating the same words.

One of the hundreds of musical arrangements Lowell Mason made used a text from Isaac Watts' hymnal. Using a melody which had been around in England for several years called, "Antioch", he made some changes to the tune, crediting it as "arranged from Handel." Part of the melody was similar to some passages within Handel's Messiah. They were combined with notes Mason wrote and repeating words in a fuging melody. The song was published in 1836 during the Christmas season. Titled "Joy to the World," the song grew to become one of the most popular Christmas carols today. Though the hymn was conceived by Isaac Watts as a song more about the Second Coming of Christ than His birth, it is beloved as a song of praise and worship today.

Joy to the world! the Lord is come

Let earth receive her King;

Let every heart prepare him room,

And heaven and nature sing,

And heaven and nature sing,

And heaven, and heaven, and nature sing.

Joy to the world! the Savior reigns;

Let men their songs employ;

While fields and floods, rocks, hills, and plains

Repeat the sounding joy,

Repeat the sounding joy,

Repeat, repeat the sounding joy.

No more let sins and sorrows grow,

Nor thorns infest the ground;

He comes to make His blessings flow

Far as the curse is found,

Far as the curse is found,

Far as, far as, the curse is found.

He rules the world with truth and grace,

And makes the nations prove

The glories of His righteousness,

And wonders of His love,

And wonders of His love,

And wonders, wonders, of His love.

Sources:

https://en.wikipedia.org/wiki/Lowell_Mason

https://www.classicfm.com/discover-music/occasions/christmas/joy-to-the-world-hymn-carol-lyrics-composer/

https://www.umcdiscipleship.org/resources/history-of-hymns-joy-to-the-world

https://en.wikipedia.org/wiki/Isaac_Watts

https://www.powerofchange.org/blog/2011/12/16/isaac-watts-joy-to-the-world.html

Blankets and Socks

Mrs. S.C. Law was a southern woman from Memphis, Tennessee. She was so proud when her only son enlisted in the Confederate Army in 1861. To support the war effort, Mrs. Law volunteered at the "Southern Mother's Hospital", caring for injured and sick soldiers. She began taking clothes and other supplies directly to the troops in 1862. When the city of Memphis fell to the Union Army, she made her way south to Georgia, where she continued to help care for the wounded in different hospitals. It was her mission to do all she could to support the Confederate States and the brave soldiers who fought for the South. Many years after the war ended, Mrs. Law wrote of her Christmas mission to help the troops.

It was a December night in 1863 in Columbus, Georgia. Mrs. Law could not sleep. She had just learned that Confederate soldiers in General J.E. Johnston's divisions were in a terrible, destitute condition. They were suffering because of the cold weather and lack of blankets to keep them warm. In fact, thousands of soldiers were having to stay up all night, sleepless, and huddled around a fire to keep warm. She greatly esteemed the soldiers' mission to protect the southern women and children from the enemy invaders from the north.

The next morning, she went to the Ladies' Aid Society in Columbus and petitioned for them to make blankets for these brave men. She said that if they would furnish blankets, she would personally take them to Dalton, Georgia and distribute them to the soldiers. In one week, several large boxes were packed to supply the Confederate soldiers with 100 blankets, 300 pairs of socks, and several boxes of underclothing. The women also generously packed Christmas boxes filled with all sorts of food that the men could only dream of – chicken, ham, sausages, butter, pickles, bread, and cake.

Accompanied by another woman from the Ladies' Aid Society, and her twelve-year-old nephew (who on getting back to Columbus ran away to the army), Mrs. Law traveled by train to Dalton, where she met her friend, Dr. John Erskine. He arranged for the party and supplies to be taken to his headquarters, at the home of a woman in the area. A courier and carriage were supplied for her use and her first visit was to the 154th Regiment. She met with a group of officers and was overwhelmed by what she learned. "General Hardee said that he had in his division fifteen hundred men without a blanket; General Hindman, one thousand; General Cheatham, hundreds, and many other divisions in a similar condition. General Pat Cleburne said that socks were a luxury his men did not know; he had not had a pair on for five months." The blankets and clothes which Mrs. Law brought were distributed where there was the greatest need.

Returning to Columbus, she raised $2,500 from businesses in the city to purchase jeans and coarse cloth from the factories. The Ladies' Aid Society went to work with these supplies. In addition, from their own homes, they took the last blankets from their beds, even cutting up carpets and lining them. "The women and children worked night and day, and in ten days [Mrs. Law] returned to the army in Dalton with seven large dry good boxes.... all packed with five hundred and thirty blankets and coverings, and sixteen hundred pairs of socks for the soldiers."

Because of the determination of Mrs. Law and her desire to make a difference, the morale and comfort of the men in the Confederate camps greatly improved from the generous

Christmas offering made by willing hands. She stated, "I wish history to recall, but for the generous help of the noble, patriotic women of Columbus, Georgia, I would have been powerless to have taken those needed stores of blankets and socks to our suffering soldiers."

Through the year, and especially during the Christmas season, may we follow the example of Mrs. Law and the Ladies' Aid Society, and generously give of our time and resources, following the admonition of Jesus Christ to "Go, and do thou likewise." (Luke 10:37)

Sources:

S. C. Law, *Reminiscences of the War of the Sixties between North and South,* published in 1892. Digitized and accessible through Library of Congress: *https://www.loc.gov/item/10020677/*

https://emergingcivilwar.com/2021/12/23/for-the-army-of-tennessee-christmas-boxes-blankets/

Chapter Ten

Midnight Christians

What does a heretic, anti-Semitism, a song banned by the church, and an American abolitionist have to do with a Christmas hymn? Let me tell you about how this unlikely combination led to one of our most beloved Christmas songs.

In the small town of Roquemaure, France in 1816, young Placide Cappeau and his friend were playing with a forbidden item – a gun. The fun ended when his friend accidently shot him, resulting in Placide's right hand being amputated. Not letting this disability define him, Placid followed academic pursuits and studied drawing, literature, and earned a law degree at a Paris university. Returning to his home in Roquemaure, he became a successful wine merchant and mayor, with the hobby of writing poetry.

Though born and raised as a Roman Catholic, he drifted from his religious roots, rarely attending mass and even vocally criticizing some tenants of the faith and clergy in general. It must have been a surprise to Placide Cappeau in 1847 when the priest asked him to write a poem for the Christmas Midnight Mass. On December 3rd, during a long, bumpy journey by coach to Paris, he read Luke 2 in the New Testament and used it as the framework to base his poem. By the time he arrived at his destination, the verses were complete. He titled it "Minuit, Chretiens", which translated means "Midnight Christians".

Moved by his finished product, and with the encouragement of the priest, the poet turned to his friend, composer Adophe Charles Adams, to write the music. Adams had many theatrical successes, including writing the musical scores for many operas and for the ballet Giselle. The subject matter and writing style presented him with a challenge unlike any he had before. Adams spent three weeks perfecting the beautiful piece of music. It was first performed by a female opera singer on Christmas Eve at the church in Roquemaure. The congregation loved the carol, and within a short time, it won the hearts of people all over France. The Catholic Church in France even endorsed its use in Christmas ceremonies.

Sadly, the Catholic church's approval of the song did not last. Revolution was at the door and Cappeau declared himself a socialist, often disparaging church leadership and teachings. Adolph Adams worried observers by calling "Midnight Christians" a song of a religious revolution. Officials in the Catholic Church called Placide Cappeau a socialist and a drunk heretic. There was also an unfounded rumor circulating that Adolphe Adam was Jewish - a falsehood that was perpetuated for more than a century. Of course, accuracy didn't concern the song's critics who thought calling someone Jewish was an insult.

According to the church leaders, any song attributed to two such unsavory characters should be banned in churches. In fact, an 1864 sacred music journal focusing on Catholic liturgical music said, "it would be a good thing to discard this piece whose popularity is…unhealthy. It is sung in the streets, at social gatherings, and at bars with live entertainment. It becomes debased and degenerated…". Yet, the song had entered the hearts of the people of France and was much loved, even though church authorities said it would not be tolerated in church worship.

"Midnight Christians" was imported across the Atlantic Ocean to Quebec, Canada, where it was considered a great honor to be asked to sing it in church services. In 1855, the song reached the ears of American Unitarian Minister John Sullivan Dwight. He decided to translate it into English, taking liberties in the text to align more with his own

34

religious beliefs. This version of the lyrics, matched with Adam's original music, became very popular in the United States – especially among northern abolitionists because of the lines in a verse which condemned slavery.

What is this incredible work – requested by a parish priest, written by a man branded as a heretic, composed by a musician who was subjected to anti-Semitism, and introduced to Americans to serve as a spotlight on the evils of slavery – all while telling the story of the birth of our Savior? This beloved, beautiful, inspired piece of music to celebrate the birth of our Savior is known today not as Minuit Chretiens, but as O Holy Night.

O Holy Night,

The stars are brightly shining,

It is the night of the dear Savior's birth;

Long lay the world in sin and error pining,

Till he appeared and the soul felt its worth.

A thrill of hope the weary soul rejoices,

For yonder breaks a new and glorious morn!

Chorus:

Fall on your knees,

Oh hear the angel voices!

Oh night divine!

Oh night when Christ was born.

Oh night, O holy night,

Oh night divine.

Led by the light of Faith serenely beaming;

With glowing hearts by His cradle we stand:

So, led by light of a star sweetly gleaming,

Here come the wise men from Orient land,

The King of Kings lay thus in lowly manger,

In all our trials born to be our friend;

Chorus:

Truly He taught us to love one another;

His law is love and His gospel is peace;

Chains shall He break, for the slave is our brother,

And in His name all oppression shall cease,

Sweet hymns of joy in grateful chorus raise we;

Let all within us praise His holy name!

Chorus:

Christ is the Lord, then ever! Ever praise we!

His power and glory, evermore proclaim!

His power and glory, evermore proclaim!

Sources:

https://petersanfilippo.medium.com/o-holy-night-an-atheist-an-american-christian-a-missing-hand-and-war-26875bdc83b2

https://www.americamagazine.org/arts-culture/2020/11/19/brief-history-o-holy-night-christmas-hymn-review

https://www.classicfm.com/discover-music/occasions/christmas/o-holy-night-original-lyrics-composer-recordings/

https://www.beliefnet.com/entertainment/movies/the-nativity-story/the-amazing-story-of-o-holy-night.aspx

Chapter Eleven

There Is No Peace

We live in the most troubled times of recent history. The hearts of men wax colder than they have ever been and darkness benights the minds and hearts of men the world over. The constant bombardment of media gloom steals our hope and destroys our peace, but it will not last! We have been here before.

The year 1861 was a similarly dark, troubled, and uncertain time in the United States. Civil war loomed. Contention and hate divided the nation and threats abounded. Henry Wadsworth Longfellow, the acclaimed poet, wrote. "Six states have left the Union, led by South Carolina. President Buchanan is an antediluvian, an après-moi-le-déluge President, who does not care what happens, if he only gets safely through his term. We owe the present state of things mainly to him. He has sympathized with the disunionists. It is now too late to put the fire out. We must let it burn out."

Henry opposed slavery, but he opposed civil war even more. Then came word on April 12, 1861, "News comes that Fort Sumter is attacked. And the war begins! Who can foresee the end?" Peace was shattered by cannon fire and the world as they knew it was in sudden turmoil!

Then, on July 9, 1861, Henry's beloved wife, Fanny Appleton Longfellow, was sealing some packages with hot wax when, it is reported, a match dropped to the floor and ignited her dress on fire. She ran to the study where Longfellow was and he attempted to put the fire out, but Fanny was badly burned and passed away the next day. Henry's grief was deep and prolonged, so much so that at times he feared that he would be sent to an asylum, so debilitating was it. One heavy year later, Henry wrote, "I can make no record of these days. Better leave them wrapped in silence. Perhaps someday God will give me peace."

If that were not enough, in March 1863, Henry's eldest son, Charles, age 19, boarded a train for Washington, D. C., and against his father's wishes, joined the Union Army. On December 1, 1863, Henry was sitting down to dinner at his Cambridge, Massachusetts home when he received a telegram that Charles had been severely wounded in the Battle of Mine Run. Henry quickly went south and brought his son home for what would be a lengthy recovery. Henry would summarize these days thus, "I have been through a great deal of trouble and anxiety."

It is out of this series of tragic events that on Christmas Day, 1864, that Henry Wadsworth Longfellow penned the following words:

I heard the bells on Christmas Day

Their old, familiar carols play,

And wild and sweet

The words repeat

Of peace on earth, good will to men!

I thought how, as the day had come,

The belfries of all Christendom

Had rolled along

The unbroken song

Of peace on earth, good will to men!

Till, ringing, singing on its way,

The world revolved from night to day,

A voice, a chime,

A chant sublime

Of peace on earth, good will to men!

The poem was written when the Civil War still tore at the nation's heart. When the poem was set to music in 1872, the next two stanzas of Longfellow's poem were left out as they have been in the singing of this sacred Christmas hymn ever since, but they tell the full story behind the hymn. Longfellow continued:

Then from each black, accursed mouth

The cannon thundered in the South,

And with the sound

The carols drowned

Of peace on earth, good will to men!

It was as if an earthquake rent

The hearth-stones of a continent,

And made forlorn

The households born

Of peace on earth, good will to men!

And in despair I bowed my head;

"There is no peace on earth," I said:

"For hate is strong,

And mocks the song

Of peace on earth, good-will to men!"

And it is here, like the pealing bells of Longfellow's Church, that his message sounds with ringing clarity. He concluded:

Then pealed the bells more loud and deep:

"God is not dead; nor doth he sleep!

The wrong shall fail

The right prevail,

With peace on earth, good will to men!"

And so, it will be for us! God is not dead! The wrong and all those support it, will fail, and the righteousness of Jesus Christ will prevail with peace. Have no fear!

Sources:

https://www.hymnologyarchive.com/i-heard-the-bells-on-christmas-day

https://www.battlefields.org/learn/articles/christmas-bells

https://www.mentalfloss.com/article/72869/how-civil-war-inspired-i-heard-bells-christmas-day

https://en.wikipedia.org/wiki/Henry_Wadsworth_Longfellow

https://www.thegospelcoalition.org/blogs/justin-taylor/the-story-of-pain-and-hope-behind-i-heard-the-bells-on-christmas-day/

Chapter Twelve

The Angels' Song

Have you ever been discouraged by the cares of the world? Do you get to the point where you can't listen to one more news report about the problems facing people both at home and abroad? If so, you may be able to relate to the author of a beloved Christmas song.

Edmund Hamilton Sears was born on April 6, 1810, on a farm in Sandisfield in western Massachusetts. He was the youngest of three sons of Joseph and Lucy Smith Sears, who taught him the importance of positive moral values and encouraged his love to study and learn. He had limited opportunities for regular schooling, due to his need to help with the farm work. However, he eventually was able to attend Union College, and then trained for the ministry at the Theological School in Cambridge, Massachusetts, graduating at the age of 27. He met the love of his life, Ellen Bacon, and they married in 1839. The couple wished for a quiet country life and Edmund, now called Reverend Sears, accepted a position preaching at the First Congregational Church in Wayland, Massachusetts.

Edmund and Ellen's family grew to four children, and the reality of meeting the financial needs of his growing family necessitated him accepting a position with a larger congregation in Lancaster. Reverend Sears took on more responsibility and had additional exposure to the contentious news of the nation. He was a man who thought for himself, not always following the opinions and accepted norms of some religious and community members. He courageously communicated the unpopular idea of male and female equality and condemned human slavery in any form.

Reverend Sears even told his congregation when the Fugitive Slave Law became enforced nationwide, that when human and Divine law conflicted, people must obey Divine law and declared that slavery was a crime which would reap national retribution.

Reverend Sears served the Congregational Church in Lancaster from 1840-47. News of suffering in the Mexican American War, threatening discord among the states over slavery, revolutions in some European countries, greed fed by newly discovered gold in California, and political divisiveness discouraged many people. Suffering a serious illness, followed by depression, Reverend Sears left Lancaster with his family, returning to Wayland, the place which felt like home, to rest and recover his health. The congregation in Wayland recalled him to serve as their pastor, which he did for another 17 years.

It was during Edmund Sear's recovery in December 1849, that a friend asked him to write a poem to celebrate the events of Christmas. It was later shared on Christmas Eve and published in a church periodical the following week. Edmund told a colleague and friend about his childhood home, which was within sight of the Berkshires – the tallest area in that part of the country. He said that as a youth, he imagined the hilltops touched the heavens, with the sky parting as angel messengers came to earth with messages of peace. Reverend Edmund Sears still believed in angels, and instead of focusing on the intimate events of Christ's birth in the stable, he highlighted the mission of angels proclaiming the good news.

The second verse may have had special significance to Edmund's childhood imagery, with cloven skies – meaning the sky divides in two, and the clouds parting the sky so God's angels can bring their good news to people on earth. His discouragement with the divisiveness of people in the world over the years could be compared to the great misunderstanding and senseless noise which happened in the Bible story of the Tower of Babel.

The third verse heralds the return of the Savior to earth.

It Came Upon the Midnight Clear

It came upon the midnight clear,

That glorious song of old,

From angels bending near the earth

To touch their harps of gold:

"Peace on the earth, good will to men

From heaven's all gracious King.

The world in solemn stillness lay

To hear the angels, sing.

When through the cloven skies they come,

With peaceful wings unfurled.

And still their heavenly music floats

O'er all the weary world.

Above its sad and lowly plains

They bend on hovering wing

And ever o'er its babel sounds

The blessed angels sing.

For lo! The days are hastening on,

By prophets seen of old,

When with the ever-circling years

Shall come the time foretold,

When the new heaven and earth shall own

The Prince of Peace their King,

And the whole world send back the song

Which now the angels sing.

Ten years later, Richard Storrs Willis, who studied music with Felix Mendelssohn in Germany, wrote the melody which we sing today. It is said that Reverend Sears, a modest man who preferred to lead a quiet life serving in his small parish, was uncomfortable with the public praise that his hymn generated. However, Edmund Hamilton Sears believed in angels and the truth they bring. He recognized the great need for people in his time to hear their message.

Are we listening to the angels' songs of peace today? Surely our need is as great as it was almost two centuries ago.

Sources:

https://historybecauseitshere.weebly.com/the-angels-song---it-came-upon-the-midnight-clear.html

https://hymnary.org/person/Sears_EH

https://www.hymnsandcarolsofchristmas.com/Hymns_and_Carols/Notes_On_Carols/it_came_upon_the_midnight_clear1.htm

Chapter Thirteen

A Gift to America

One of the most unique Christmas gifts to the United States happened during the holiday season of 1896. Let me tell you about a talented young man who was responsible for it.

John was born on November 6, 1854 in Washington, D.C., the immigrant son of a Portuguese father and a German mother. He grew up there during the Civil War, and as a child enjoyed hearing the military bands that filled the streets of the city. His father played the trombone and was a member of the U.S. Marine Band. In addition to attending grammar school, John was enrolled in a private conservatory of music, where he studied piano and most of the orchestral instruments, although his first love was the violin. By the age of 13, he was very proficient playing violin, and determined to join a circus band. His father learned of John's plan and put an end to it, instead enlisting him as an apprentice musician with the Marine Band, where he remained until he was 20 years old. For the next six years, John worked as a musician, composer, and proofreader, as well as playing in the orchestra with multiple traveling theater companies.

While he was on tour, John received a telegram which would shape the rest of his life. He was offered the position as leader of the Marine Band in Washington. He accepted and reported for duty on October 1, 1880, becoming the band's 17th leader.

This was John's first experience conducting a military band. He updated and made changes to the music, wrote original compositions for the group, and initiated exceptionally strict and demanding rehearsals. John had perfect pitch and the talent of reading a musical score and hearing exactly how it sounded in his head. He called it his "brain-band." As the Marine Band director, it became the premier military band in the nation, attracting enthusiastic audiences and even touring the country each year beginning in 1891. The group flourished for 12 years with John at the helm, and continues to this day as an elite band, "The President's Own". In fact, John wrote "Semper Fidelis", the official march of the Marine Corps, dedicating it to the officers and men of that branch of the military.

This successful band director was none other than John Phillip Sousa. The American bandmaster became known as the "March King" because of his many original, stirring band compositions.

In 1892, he resigned his post as director, starting his own Sousa Band. It toured the United States and Europe from 1892-1931, performing in 15,523 concerts and exposing audiences to the latest cutting-edge music, ragtime, and of course, his incomparable marches.

In December 1896, John and his wife took a well-deserved vacation in Europe. While there, he received word that the manager of his Sousa Band, David Blakely, had died. He immediately booked passage back to the United States on the ship Teutonic. As the vessel steamed out of the harbor, he began to hear a rhythmic beat of a band playing in his brain. Throughout the whole voyage, the imaginary band played the distinct melody over and over again. John said that day after day as he walked, it kept crashing into his very soul. The ship docked, and on Christmas Day, 1896, he wrote down the song that his "brain-band" had played for days, without changing even one note.

What was this Christmas gift of glorious band music? John called it "The Stars and Stripes Forever." The march was an immediate success, and Sousa's Band played it from then on at the end of almost every concert, with piccolos, trumpets, and trombones front and center on the stage. "The Stars and Stripes Forever" is considered to this day one of the finest and most patriotic marches ever written. Audiences spontaneously rise to their feet and the song often draws tears to their eyes. The words of the chorus have captured the hearts and spirit of what it means to be an American.

Hurrah for the flag of the free,

May it wave as our standard forever,

The gem of the land and the sea,

The banner of the right.

Let despots remember the day

When our fathers with mighty endeavor,

Proclaimed as they marched to the fray,

That by their might, and by their right,

It waves forever!

On December 11, 1987, "The Stars and Stripes Forever" was designated as the national march of the United States. John Phillip Sousa's Christmas gift to America more than 100 years ago continues to be an integral part of the celebration of American life. Thank you, Mr. Sousa, and Merry Christmas.

Sources:

https://www.americaslibrary.gov/aa/sousa/aa_sousa_forever_1.html

https://www.songfacts.com/facts/john-philip-sousa/the-stars-and-stripes-forever

https://www.marineband.marines.mil/About/Our-History/John-Philip-Sousa/

Chapter Fourteen

Christmas Morning

The lyrics and melody of a hymn have the power to unite and comfort believers – even in the most unlikely places. This was the case with a hymn first published in England in 1787.

On Christmas Eve in 1898, a memorable moment in time touched the lives of United States soldiers who were serving in the Spanish-American War. Northerners and Southerners, blacks and whites served together on the island of Cuba, more than thirty years after the United States Civil War. Lieutenant-Colonel Curtis Guild, Jr. was serving as Inspector-General of the Seventh Army Corps near Havana and described this incident.

It was a balmy, tropical night, and he, like many of his comrades, were talking of Christmas and home. Memories of family, sweethearts, and the celebrations of the season were surely part of their conversations. As the clock struck twelve to welcome Christmas Day, from the camp of the Forty-Ninth Iowa came a sentinel's call, "Number ten; twelve o'clock and all's well!"

The sentinel's call had barely finished, when from the bandsmen's tents of the same regiment there arose the music of an old, familiar hymn. This hymn, which first made its way to America from England in 1820, was frequently sung in many Christian churches. Northern soldiers would have learned this song as children, from their mothers. To Southern soldiers, it was not only a beloved song, but the favorite hymn of General Robert E. Lee, and was sung at his funeral.

A single baritone voice started the song. Another voice joined in, and soon the whole regiment was singing – the Sixth Missouri followed, then the Fourth Virginia, and soon all of the rest of the army spanning the ridges of the camp. However, the song was not one of the popular Christmas carols of the day, but the words written more than 100 years earlier by a believer only identified as "K---", who trusted in God and His promises. All of the verses would have been familiar to most of these men, but this verse particularly was mentioned by Lieutenant-Colonel Guild.

Fear not, I am with thee, O be not dismayed;

For I am thy God, and will still give thee aide;

I'll strengthen thee, help thee, and cause thee to stand,

Upheld by My righteous, omnipotent hand.

The hymn, How Firm a Foundation, brought comfort and unity to American soldiers that Christmas morning. It has been published in over 1,900 hymnals and provided consolation and hope to Christians for over 200 years. The final verse states:

The soul that on Jesus hath leaned for repose

I will not, I cannot, desert to his foes;

That soul, though all hell should endeavor to shake,

I'll never, no never, no never forsake!

Sources:

https://hymnary.org/text/how_firm_a_foundation_ye_saints_of

https://reasonabletheology.org/hymn-story-how-firm-a-foundation/

Benson, L. F. 1903. Studies of Familiar Hymns. Philadelphia, The Westminster Press.

https://books.google.com/books?id=o5ECAAAAYAAJ&printsec=titlepage&sourc e=gbs_summary_r&cad=0#v=onepage&q&f=false

http://iagenweb.org/plymouth/Military/SpAm_ClaggBen.html

Chapter Fifteen

Truce

In 1783, one of America's Founding Fathers, Benjamin Franklin, wrote, "There never was a good war or a bad peace." Unfortunately, over 200 years later, some countries and people of the world have not embraced this idea. The news all too often is about war in different parts of the world and the inhumanity of the soldiers who have been drawn into the conflict. However, there have been some times in the Christmas season when soldiers on opposing sides have shown their humanity and longing for the elusive goal of peace.

World War I began in late July 1914, and quickly escalated. Germany, Austria-Hungary, Bulgaria, and their colonies, known as the Central Powers, were pitted against France, the United Kingdom, Russia, Italy, Japan, United States, and their allies, known as the Allied Powers. The two sides engaged in brutal trench warfare. In the earliest weeks of the war, both sides were hostile and angry. By December, the soldiers, who had expected a quick end to the war, were exhausted and had seen much destruction and death. On December 7, 1914, Pope Benedict XV called for a temporary ceasefire for Christmas, so the guns would be silent on the night of Christ's birth. The plea was officially ignored.

Without the sanction of their generals or High Command, soldiers from both sides of the conflict, in different areas, took matters into their own hands. A brief, spontaneous cease-fire spread up and down the Western Front. It has been estimated that up to 100,000 troops laid down their weapons in the informal interruption of hostility. Letters written home by the soldiers told what happened in different parts of the Western Front.

"We were in the trenches on Christmas Eve, and about 8:30 in the evening the firing was almost at a standstill. Then the Germans started shouting across to us, 'a happy Christmas' and commenced putting up lots of Christmas trees with hundreds of candles on the parapets of their trenches." – Cpl. Leon Harris, 13th Battalion, London Regiment.

In one area along the line, British soldiers reported that the two sides serenaded each other with carols – the Germans sang "Silent Night" and the British sang a chorus of "The First Noel."

Graham Williams of the Fifth London Brigade wrote the following: "First the Germans would sing one of their carols and then we would sing one of ours, until when we started up 'O Come, All Ye Faithful' the Germans immediately joined in singing the same hymn to the Latin words "Adeste Fideles." And I thought, well, this is really the most extraordinary thing – two nations both singing the same carol in the middle of a war."

"We would sing a song or a carol first and then they would sing one and I tell you they can harmonize all right…On Christmas Day, we came to an armistice between ourselves without any permission and you could see us and the Germans shaking hands, talking, and even exchanging names, cards, and cigarettes…Everyone that I spoke to said that he had enough of the war and wished himself [to go] home again. There were a good many amongst them that could speak broken English all right and they said 'you make it no shoot, we make it not shoot.'"

– Pvt. G. Layton, A Company, 2st Royal Warwickshire Regiment

German Lieutenant Kurt Zehmisch, a member of the 134 Saxon infantry, was a schoolteacher who was fluent in both English and German. In his personal diary he wrote: "Eventually, the English brought a soccer ball from their trenches, and pretty soon a lively game ensued. How marvelously wonderful, yet how strange it was. The English officers felt the same way about it. Thus Christmas, the celebration of love, managed to bring mortal enemies together as friends for a time." In many other locations there were accounts of having kickabout matches or informal soccer games in the no man's land between opposing trenches.

A German Lieutenant, Johannes Niemann, wrote "[I] grabbed my binoculars and looking cautiously over the parapet saw the incredible sight of our soldier exchanging cigarettes, schnapps, and chocolate with the enemy."

Bruce Bairnsfather, a British soldier, reported, "The last I saw was one of my machine gunners, who was a bit of an amateur hairdresser in civil life, cutting the unnaturally long hair of a German who was patiently kneeling on the ground whilst the automatic clippers crept up the back of his neck." A couple of German soldiers even asked the British to mail letters they had written to girlfriends in Liverpool and London. In many locations, both sides buried their dead who had fallen in the No Man's Land between the trenches.

The soldiers from both sides learned that the enemy they were fighting were much like themselves. They had mothers, sweethearts, wives, and other family waiting to welcome them home.

In a 1930 interview, one British soldier, Murdoch M. Woods, summed up his feelings that were shared by many on both sides of the conflict. He said, "I came to the conclusion that I have held very firmly ever since, that if we had been left to ourselves there would never have been another shot fired."

The news media became aware of the Christmas truce through letters which soldiers wrote home and many first-hand accounts were published. Though the war continued for three more years, the opposing forces had been humanized. The Allied and Central Commands took steps to be sure another unauthorized truce would not happen again. Soldiers were reminded that communicating and fraternizing with the enemy was forbidden and would be considered an act of treason.

The Christmas Truce of 1914 is a reminder that as part of the human family, we share many of the same hopes and dreams. In Matthew 7:12 the Savior said, "…all things whatsoever ye would that men should do to you, do ye even so to them…". May we all make a greater effort to follow the words of the heavenly host on the night of Christ's birth, and strive for "peace, good will toward men."

Sources:

http://exhibitions.theworldwar.org/christmas-truce/incidents/14/wonderful-christmas-exonian-tells-of-christmas-trees-before-the-trenches

http://exhibitions.theworldwar.org/christmas-truce/incidents/123/pretty-decent-in-the-trenches-a-birmingham-soldiers-christmas-experience

https://www.washingtonpost.com/news/retropolis/wp/2017/12/24/the-christmas-truce-miracle-soldiers-put-down-their-guns-to-sing-carols-and-drink-wine/

https://www.history.com/topics/christmas-truce-1914-world-war-i-soldier-accounts

https://www.smithsonianmag.com/history/the-story-of-the-wwi-christmas-truce-11972213/

Regan, Geoffrey. Military Anecdotes (1992) p. 139, Guinness Publishing ISBN 0-85112-519-0

https://time.com/3643889/christmas-truce-1914/

Chapter Sixteen

A Christmas Eve to Remember

To befriend the one who regards himself as your enemy is the heart of true religion. The actions of a German woman and her son who lived in a forest cottage on the German-Belgium border exemplified this. It was Christmas Eve 1944, and Allied and German soldiers were fighting nearby in a campaign we know as the Battle of the Bulge.

After dark, there was a knock on the door, and Mrs. Vicken nervously answered. Three American soldiers, the enemy, stood there with their weapons. One man was seriously wounded. She motioned they could enter the cottage, where they laid the wounded man on her twelve-year-old son Fritz's bed. Not speaking English, she communicated with one soldier who spoke a little French. She tended to the wounded fighter, giving instructions to her son to help the others take off their wet jackets and boots. With their uniforms off, they looked and acted just like any young men. Mrs. Vicken told her son to fetch potatoes and the plump rooster they had been raising for a holiday meal. Fritz and one of the soldiers prepared the food.

There was another knock on the door, and Mrs. Vicken answered, expecting to see more Americans. Instead, there were four German soldiers standing there. All German citizens knew that harboring enemy soldiers was considered high treason. Stepping outside, she wished them a Merry Christmas. They explained that they had lost their company and would like to rest in the cottage until morning. She summoned her composure and invited them to share their meal – with a condition. She explained that she had three guests who they may not consider friends, and sternly told them that it was Christmas Eve and there would be peace in her home. She explained that both groups were lost from their comrades, hungry, cold, and tired. For this Christmas Eve, there was no need for fighting. The German soldiers were told to put their weapons outside by the woodpile, and the Americans did so, too.

Though the men regarded each other with distrust, they sat down where Mrs. Vicken asked. After cooking more potatoes, the six soldiers, Mrs. Vicken, and Fritz enjoyed a Christmas Eve meal. Before eating, she offered a prayer asking Jesus to be their guest. This brought tears to the eyes of everyone. Two of the German soldiers even produced a bottle of wine and loaf of rye bread to add to the meal.

In the morning, the German soldiers gave the Americans directions on how to get back to their units, and Mrs. Vicken gave the GIs her best tablecloth to use with two poles to make a stretcher to carry the wounded soldier. The brave German mother then instructed all of the soldiers to use care so they could return to their families and wished them the blessings of God. The German and American soldiers shook hands and walked away in opposite directions.

Mrs. Vicken befriended those in need, whether friend or foe, and taught her son and the soldiers that enemies can become friends. In 2 Thessalonians 3: 15-16 it says, "Yet count him not as an enemy, but admonish him as a brother. Now the Lord… give you peace [and] be with you all."

Sources:
https://thechaplainkit.com/2017/12/24/truce-in-the-forest-the-story-of-a-world-war-ii-truce-between-german-american-soldiers-during-the-battle-
Vincken, Fritz, "Truce in the Forest," Readers Digest, January 1973, pp 111-114.

Chapter Seventeen

A Soldier's Song

During World War II, there was hardly a home in the country that didn't have a family member serving in the Armed Forces. In fact, by September 1945, over twelve million Americans were in military service, representing more than nine percent of the U.S. population. It is no wonder that a song written in 1943 by Walter Kent and James Gannon, and performed by Bing Crosby, became an instant hit that holiday season. Written from the viewpoint of a member of the Armed Forces who was away from home for the holidays, it touched a tender place in the hearts of Americans, both GIs and civilians. The soldier in the song promised that he'd be home for Christmas, "if only in my dreams." The song was titled "I'll Be Home for Christmas."

Although the music and words were beloved by U.S. soldiers and families alike, the B.B.C. in the United Kingdom banned it from their playlist for the duration of the war, at the urging of military officials. They worried that it would just make their troops depressed and distracted. However, "I'll Be Home for Christmas" became the most requested song at American Christmas U.S.O. shows in both Europe and the Pacific, and when Bing Crosby did performances for the troops, no matter what the month of the year, they demanded that he sing that song.

In the same year "I'll Be Home for Christmas" was released, the sailors on the battleship U.S.S. North Carolina had a memorable experience which represented the feelings expressed in the song. In August 1943, Chaplain E.P. Wuebbens, who served the 2,300 servicemen on the ship, wanted to do something to raise the morale of the men. Many of his crew were fathers and brothers who would be spending the Christmas holiday thousands of miles away from their families. Of his crew, 147 had sons or daughters and 582 had brothers and sisters. Wuebbens collected $5.00 from every crew member who had a young family at home, collecting $2,404.25.

Chaplain Wuebbens then wrote a letter, and a check for the amount collected, to Macy's Department Store in New York City. He requested that the store use the money to purchase, wrap, and mail a toy to each of the 729 children on the list. He allotted $3.00 each for a toy and $2.00 for shipping and a card. Whether a football, Raggedy Ann doll, stuffed animal, board game, book, or other toy was sent, the card was to say, "Merry Christmas from your dad/brother and his shipmates in the U.S.S. North Carolina!" The last paragraph of the letter the chaplain wrote said: "We realize that we are asking a great deal, but your firm gave this ship such splendid service a few years ago that we have all confidence that you can and will again. You will be adding greatly to the happiness of our children and to our own Christmas joy out here in one of the war zones. Incidentally, we hope that a bit of that joy will reflect on you and your staff of workers."

Macy's Department store fulfilled their order, but in addition to sending gifts to the military families at home, they made a one of a kind gift for the soldiers as well. They reached out to each family and asked if they wanted to come to the Macy's store and send a special message to their loved one who would not be able to be home for Christmas. Many mothers and children came and were filmed opening their gifts and telling their husbands and brothers hello and Merry Christmas.

On Christmas Eve 1943, in the New Hebrides Islands of the South Pacific, the men on the U.S.S. North Carolina watched their fellow crew members perform in a variety show which included Christmas music, songs, and skits. When the entertainment ended, Chaplin Wuebbens turned on the film projector. Expecting to see a training video or other movie they had already watched, the soldiers were overwhelmed when they saw their wives, children, and loved ones appear before them on the screen, expressing their love and holiday wishes. The tough sailors watched with tears streaming down their faces. They weren't home for Christmas, but a bit of home had come to them.

On Christmas morning, the U.S.S. North Carolina, who earned 15 battle stars in WWII, shipped out, with orders to provide support for a carrier attack. Thanks to Macy's Department Store, the fathers, husbands, and brothers aboard the ship were able to experience the sights and sounds of Christmas, in a more wonderful way than they could have dreamed.

Sources:

https://www.starnewsonline.com/picture-gallery/news/local/2015/12/14/christmas-aboard-the-uss-north/913064007/

https://blog.coldwellbanker.com/the-story-of-ill-be-home-for-christmas-and-the-battleship-north-carolina/

https://toritto.wordpress.com/2018/12/17/the-battleship-north-carolina-macys-and-christmas-1943/

https://www.ourstate.com/christmas-aboard-the-uss-north-carolina/

https://www.cheatsheet.com/entertainment/why-bing-crosbys-ill-be-home-for-christmas-was-banned-by-the-bbc-during-world-war-ii.html/

https://www.loc.gov/item/ihas.200000010/

Chapter Eighteen

Hope for the Holidays

Our country owes a huge debt to the men and women in the Armed Forces. Being away from home and family is especially challenging for deployed service members, and at Christmas time, it is even more difficult. To help support these troops, the USO (United Service Operations) was founded in 1941 after the attack on Pearl Harbor and when the U.S. joined World War II. This is the story of one man who partnered with the USO to bring hope for the holidays to the troops for over 50 years.

Born to British parents in England in 1903, Leslie Townes Hope was the fifth of seven children. The family emigrated to Ohio in 1908. Growing up, he learned to sing, dance, and do impersonations. He dropped out of school at the age of 16, working different part-time jobs. For a short time, he was a boxer, going by the name of "Packy East." Later, he officially changed his name to "Lester Hope," and he worked as a variety stage entertainer in Vaudeville and then on Broadway. Finally, after he had achieved considerable success on the stage, he began using the name that the world would come to know as – Bob Hope – one of the most popular comedians and entertainers of his time.

In the mid-1930's, he embraced entertaining on the radio, and launched the popular, long-running The Bob Hope Show. Then in 1938, he made his first of over 50 full-length feature films, in which he sang the song which would become his signature tune – "Thanks for the Memory." Bob Hope became famous and Americans adored him.

When the United States joined their allies in World War II, Bob Hope tried to enlist in the military, but was told he could make a greater impact as an entertainer. He joined with the USO in performing for troops at home and overseas. His first show for a soldier audience was in 1941 in California, and he later said, "I looked at them, they laughed at me, and it was love at first sight."

During that war, Hope performed USO shows not only in the United States, but also in Europe and the South Pacific. In fact, in 1944 alone, he traveled 30,000 miles, going between islands in the South Pacific, putting on more than 150 shows for the troops. He traveled overseas six times, logging more than a million miles during WWII. Bob Hope was often in dangerous areas. The groups of GIs he put on shows for made him a first-rate military target, and even the Nazis tried to track his shows in Europe. They bombed three different towns while he was the entertainer there!

World War II ended, but his commitment to the USO did not. He continued to do shows and visit Veterans hospitals. In December 1948, Bob Hope, and other performers, traveled to Berlin, Germany to entertain the forces helping in the Berlin Airlift. This was his first Christmas tour to entertain troops and the beginning of a tradition each December that lasted until 1990.

In 1964, Bob Hope and company made the first of nine USO trips to Vietnam. He made annual holiday trips there through 1972. The main purpose of his Christmas shows in Vietnam was to show support for the troops and raise their morale. On each trip, he brought along singers, dancers, comedians, and a band. His troupe included major celebrities and stars of the day. There was often danger involved in their visits. While performing in Saigon in 1967, the Viet Cong initiated a terrorist attack against him and his group at their hotel, missing them by 10 minutes. It was not unusual for the enemy to fire on or attack a base shortly after a show ended.

For many service members, watching a live Bob Hope
USO Christmas show was the highlight of the deployment.
Bob Hope once said, "If you can get a joke to penetrate
a helmet, or a bulletproof vest, and the punchline to stay
in somebody's mind…make them laugh, and forget about
their predicament, even for a few seconds, to me it's a good
achievement for a comedian."

At the end of each performance on the 1964 Vietnam tour,
a chaplain would offer a prayer and then Anita Bryant ended
the show by singing the first verse of "Silent Night." The
troops and performers were then asked to join in on the
second verse. Bob Hope was mindful of the men who could
not attend the live performances. Veteran Donald Scott told
of working as an aerial port duty officer during the show. That
evening, Hope's plane took off to the next destination. The
soldiers called his plane and were able to speak to Bob. Scott
recalled, "He summoned Anita Bryant to the microphone,
and she sang 'Silent Night' [to them] as they flew through
the dark, black skies of Vietnam. I will never forget this act of
kindness for a small group of about five guys who could not
attend the big show."

Letters which soldiers wrote home showed how much
they valued seeing the performances. Private First Class
Christopher Ammons wrote the following: "I couldn't really
believe it. There was Bob Hope right in front of me cracking
jokes…at the end of the show we all sang Silent Night with
the stars [performers]." He also hoped that the television
cameras would include his image so his family could see him
on the annual NBC specials which were broadcast later in the
United States.

A Navy Seabee, Russell Hohl, told how he and two other GIs
worked extra hard for two weeks so they could take a full day
off for the show. They got to the site early and had close spots,
about 20 feet from the stage. After sitting there all day, he

64

wrote that "several MPs [military policemen] showed up with a bunch of officers and forced them to move so the officers could take their prime spots." In spite of having to move to less desirable seating, Hohl said the show was the "high point of my two tours in Vietnam." Bob Hope would not have approved of replacing enlisted men with officers, preferring that the seats closest to the stage be given to enlisted troops, straight from the field, and hospital patients who were able to attend.

Seabee Ron Ronning saw Hope's final USO show of the Vietnam War. He said, "He brought such enthusiasm, brought your life back to you. You felt like you were renewed. That was one of the biggest thrills of my life."

A generation after the Vietnam War, Bob Hope's final USO Christmas Shows were held for troops deployed to Operation Desert Shield and Operation Desert Storm. Again, these service men and women said that seeing Bob Hope in person was the highlight of their tour of duty. One veteran, John R. Rogers, recalled that his whole unit was invited to the unexpected show. He said, "Most of us had fathers and/ or grandfathers who saw the Bob Hope show during war-time and we felt that we now shared something special with them…It made my Christmas."

Bob Hope traveled to more war zones than even some of the highest-ranking military leaders of all time, bringing a piece of home and hope to the front lines for over 50 years. He headlined 57 USO tours, performing on military bases around the world, in war zones near the front lines, and on ships at sea. He never served in the Armed Forces of the United States himself. In 1997, a Joint Resolution of Congress named Leslie Townes (Bob) Hope the "first and only honorary veteran of the U.S. Armed Forces." After receiving this, Bob Hope said, "I've been given many awards in my lifetime – but to be numbered among the men and women I admire most — is the greatest honor I have ever received."

Perhaps a letter written during World War II by Wm. H. Ingram, Captain USMC, speaks for all his comrades through the years that benefited from Bob Hope's service. He said:

"Dear Bob, there isn't a guy, Army, Navy, or Marines, that will ever sell you short. You may be a comedian…but Mister, you very often hit the nail on the head. Sir, we appreciate it, believe me."

Is there a lesson from Bob Hope's life of service, not only during the holidays, but throughout the year? Part of Revelation 2:19 in the New Testament says: "I know thy works, and charity, and service, and faith, and thy patience…". May we find ways to be true Christians and give others "hope for the holidays", following the example of Bob Hope.

Sources:

https://blog.theveteranssite.greatergood.com/bob-hope-uso/

https://www.loc.gov/wiseguide/aug08/bobhope.html

https://www.historynet.com/bob-hopes-vietnam-christmas-tours/

https://www.uso.org/stories/2575-veterans-share-memories-of-bob-hope-uso-christmas-shows

https://www.arts.gov/stories/magazine/2012/2/soul-america/lifting-spirits

https://www.wearethemighty.com/mighty-history/bob-hope-uso-military/

LEGISLATIVE HISTORY—H.J. Res. 75: HOUSE REPORTS: No. 105–109 (Comm. on Veterans' Affairs). CONGRESSIONAL RECORD, Vol. 143 (1997): June 3, considered and passed House. Sept. 9, considered and passed Senate. WEEKLY COMPILATION OF PRESIDENTIAL DOCUMENTS, Vol. 33 (1997): Oct. 30, Presidential statement.

Chapter Nineteen

Dreaming of Christmas

There are some Christmas songs which seem to take on a life of their own, adding to the rich traditions of the holiday season. This is the story of such a song and the man who wrote it.

In 1888, in Mogilev, Russia, a son was born to Moses and Lena Beilin. They called him Israel Isidore Beilin. As an adult, Israel admitted to no memories of his first five years living in Russia, except one – when he was lying on a blanket by the side of the road, watching his house burn to the ground. You see, the family was Jewish and the target of discrimination and brutal pogroms. Like hundreds of thousands of Russian Jewish families, they emigrated to the United States. After their arrival in 1893, the family settled in the Lower East Side of New York. Their last name was changed to "Baline" and young Israel was called "Izzy." The family members all worked, pooling their meager salaries. Izzy was able to go to school until his father died when he was 13. That was the end of his formal education.

Izzy worked selling newspapers outside of busy saloons and restaurants in New York and enjoyed hearing music coming from these buildings. He learned if he sang some of the songs he'd heard while selling papers, people would toss him a few coins. At the age of 14, he left home and lived with other young immigrants. He soon realized that he was the most successful when singing well-known tunes which expressed simple sentiments. At the age of 18, he became a singing waiter, delighting customers with songs he made up. Izzy had no formal musical training, but in his free time after hours at the Pelham Café, he taught himself to play the piano and improvise. However, he only learned to play the piano in one key, F sharp, and never was able to read or write music notes.

In 1907, Izzy sold the publishing rights for his first song to a music publisher for 75 cents. Because he co-wrote the song with a pianist, he only received half of the payment for the piece. The Jewish immigrant with limited education and no formal music training continued to write songs, and in 1911, a dance song he wrote, "Alexander's Ragtime Band," topped the charts and sold more than a million copies of sheet music.

On the first song he published, Izzy began using a pen name which closely resembled his birth name, but sounded less ethnic. In 1911, he legally changed his name from Izzy Baline to Irving Berlin. He is known today as one of the greatest songwriters of his time. During his 60-year career, he wrote hundreds of songs, including music for 20 Broadway shows and 15 Hollywood films. "There's No Business-Like Show Business" and "God Bless America" are two of the songs he wrote which are still well known today.

One of the ironies of music history is that a Jewish immigrant, who celebrated the holiday of Hanukkah in December, wrote the best-selling Christmas song of all time. Irving had moved with his family from New York to Southern California, and wrote a Christmas song from the viewpoint of someone who was missing cold, winter weather during the holiday season. Instead of white snow outside, there was green grass, sunshine, and palm trees. The words told of someone dreaming of a white Christmas with snow, sleigh bells, children, and Christmas greetings. It ended with the wish that your days would be merry and "all your Christmases be white". He called the song "White Christmas." It was first heard on a radio show called The Kraft Music Hall, on Christmas Day in 1941. The entertainer who sang "White Christmas" was Bing Crosby.

Christmas 1941 was a somber time for the United States. The Japanese attack on Pearl Harbor had happened 18 days before. Bing Crosby recorded the song for distribution in 1942, and by the following Christmas, young American troops found themselves overseas at war during the holidays. Armed Forces radio played "White Christmas" many times daily, as it reminded the troops of home.

Bing Crosby traveled overseas many times during the war to entertain the soldiers. No matter what month of the year or where in the world he went, the song was always the most requested, in spite of Bing's hesitation to perform it. Not wanting to make the men sad, he tried to cut it out of the shows – but the GIs just hollered their request until he sang it. By the end of the war, "White Christmas" was the best-selling song of all time and kept that distinction for 56 years.

"White Christmas" was featured in two full length movies. In 1942, it was sung in the movie Holiday Inn, and Irving Berlin later won an Academy Award for the song. During the 1943 awards ceremony, Berlin was a presenter and ended up awkwardly announcing himself as the winner. In 1954, the song was the title track of another Bing Crosby musical called White Christmas.

In the last days of April 1975, "White Christmas" played a part in another war. The U.S. military was in the final phase in the evacuation of American civilians and "at-risk" Vietnamese from Saigon, South Vietnam, before the takeover of the city by the North Vietnamese People's Army. The American Embassy issued a secret evacuation signal to notify people when to assemble at designated locations for helicopter pick up. When the evacuation was ordered, the code would be broadcast on Armed Forces Radio. It was: "The temperature in Saigon is 105 degrees and rising. This will be followed by the playing of "I'm Dreaming of a White Christmas." As helicopters arrived to pick up people at the American

Embassy, "White Christmas" could be heard playing on the radios.

Christmas did have special significance to Irving Berlin – but not in the way you would expect. He was a dedicated husband and father. His wife, Ellin, had been raised as a Catholic, and the family recognized holidays from both faiths. His second child of four, and only son, was born in early December 1928. They named him Irving Berlin, Jr. Just three weeks later, on Christmas Day, his name sake died. December 25th became a day of grief and remembrance. Every year after the death of their son, the family would visit his grave on Christmas Day. When the family relocated from New York to California, visiting Irving Jr. 's resting place was not possible. Perhaps that was one reason that "White Christmas" was a more somber song.

At Irving Berlin's 100th birthday tribute, one year before his death, news anchor Walter Cronkite said that Berlin "helped write the story of this country, capturing the best of who we are and the dreams that shape our lives." The song "White Christmas" has shared the best and worst of times with Irving Berlin and the people of his adopted country for over eighty years, and will continue to be woven into the memories of our life stories every Christmas season.

Sources:

https://en.wikipedia.org/wiki/Irving_Berlin

https://historydaily.org/white-christmas-facts-stories-trivia

https://www.countryliving.com/life/news/a45720/white-christmas-song-history/

https://en.wikipedia.org/wiki/Operation_Frequent_Wind

https://www.mentalfloss.com/article/79412/11-ritzy-facts-about-irving-berlin

https://www.kuow.org/stories/sad-story-behind-white-christmas-america-s-favorite-christmas-carol

Chapter Twenty

A Letter From Dad

It's Christmas time, and you know, this time of year our minds are focused so much on the gifts we need to buy for the ones we love. Well, in light of that, may I share something that happened not too long ago?

I came home from work after a busy day. I went upstairs and dropped my stuff – and then I noticed on my pillow a note, and it was written on that kind of paper, that unique kind of paper, that told me it came from my youngest daughter. I opened it up, and sure enough, it was a note from Shaina.

It said, "Dear Daddy, I miss you. I'm having fun here at school … Can I go to Santa's secret shop? You're gone too much. You are the best daddy in the whole world. Love, Shaina."

Talk about a payday—I loved it! I called her to me, knelt down on her level, and thanked her for the wonderful note. When I told her I loved her too, she threw her arms around my neck and just hugged me tight. It was a wonderful and tender moment.

Now, a few days later, I was with a group of teenagers.

We were chatting casually when, out of genuine curiosity, I asked them, "If you could have anything for Christmas and money was not a consideration, what would it be?"

Well, I have to confess here my shallowness. I expected them to start rambling off all these expensive toys that they would like to have. To be honest, a few of them did mention some toys they'd like to have. But many, if not most of them, wanted such things as their families home for the holidays.

They wanted to spend time with their families and share experiences with their loved ones. I was surprised by that. I was impressed by that.

One young woman's answer stood out in particular.

In response to the question, she said, "Well, I'd want some money for Christmas, and then I'd want a letter from my dad." Well, the money answer I expected, but the letter from dad – I was taken back by that, and I asked her why she would want that. I mean, I figured of all things that a teenager would want least from her parents, a sentimental letter would be the last thing.

Well, she explained that her father, at least once a year, writes her a letter in which he opens his heart, and tells her that he loves her. The letters have become a cherished tradition for her. In them, Dad shares his faith, tells of experiences in his own life, gives her guidance, and tells her what he expects from her.

I couldn't believe what I was hearing.

"You mean to tell me, of all the things you could have, you would most want a letter from your dad?"

"Yes," she said, and she meant it!

You know something? Maybe our loved ones really don't want the gifts that come out of stores this year as much as they want the gifts that come out of the heart—the gifts of memories. Cherish your family and let them know how much you love and value them.

A Piano For Christmas

I would like to tell you the story of two pianos which have had special meaning in my life. From the time I was a toddler, there were many photos taken of me sitting at a piano trying to play it. That upright "Hobart M Cable" piano was a gift from my grandparents, Ray and Bessie Johansen, to my mom after she was married. They said they wanted their future grandchildren to be able to learn to play the piano, and my mom determined that the generous gift would be put to good use. I was the oldest in the family, followed by three sisters.

My mother was my first piano teacher and I welcomed the idea of taking piano lessons with anticipation and excitement. Like most kids, my eagerness was soon tempered by the fact that to have success playing, hours of practice are required. We were living in Soda Springs, Idaho and in a few months, Mrs. Murdoch became my teacher, followed by Mrs. Willie when we moved to a different state.

The rule in my house was that piano lessons were a requirement for every child. Practicing the piano for lessons was also required – not optional. The time came when all four of us were taking piano lessons. My mom would often sit at the end of the bench, insisting that we count and play rhythm and notes correctly. Sometimes there were battles and tears over practicing, but in the end, my mom won what we affectionately call "the piano wars" and all was well. With four kids taking piano lessons, my grandparents' gift was played constantly.

As I entered high school, I found I enjoyed playing piano the most when I could play what I wanted, the way I wanted. When practicing, I would often play parts of what Mozart,

Beethoven, or Rachmaninoff had written and part of what I made up to sound the way I thought it should sound. However, in addition to playing piano and singing in a choir, I found I had an affinity for activities like school swim team, diving team, soccer, and rock climbing. There wasn't enough time for me to do everything I liked, and at the end of 10th grade I convinced my parents to let me quit piano lessons.

During the next year, I would play the piano a little, but without any goals or expectations, my progress stalled. Along the way, I made a life changing discovery – playing piano was a part of me and I missed it! At the beginning of 12th grade, I talked my piano teacher into letting me take lessons again and committed to my parents that I would make time to practice. Along with assigned lessons, I started writing piano songs, and even won a school contest for a duet I had written. I began to make frequent trips to the local piano store to play their new, digital pianos which could record the songs I played.

As Christmas approached in my freshman year of university, I dreamed of saving enough money for a digital piano. It would take years to save enough money from my part-time lifeguard job, not to mention needing money to pay college fees. My parents both worked, but with four children, ages 11-18, there was not a lot of extra money for things we didn't need. That year, in December 1997, they probably planned to spend no more than $600 on gifts for everyone for Christmas. There was no way they could spend $5,000 for a digital piano for me. It just wasn't realistic, and we all know that pianos are far too heavy to be pulled in a sleigh and fit down a chimney.

On Christmas morning, the family awoke to presents and the excitement of unwrapping gifts. There was no piano under the tree that morning. In fact, the gifts I received seemed to be particularly underwhelming when compared to my three sisters. I got a music book and a harmonica – and a shirt and tie. The "dad gift" we all joked about was my reality!

When all hope was nearly lost, my father pulled an envelope out from behind the tree and said, "Jason, it looks like this has your name on it." I opened the envelope and began to read the note. It said to walk down the basement hall and go into the empty room next to mine. My parents and siblings followed me down the hall, and I opened the door to the unfinished room with the cement floor. In the corner, there was a digital piano – the exact one that I had dreamed about playing and recording music on! Somehow the piano had been delivered days earlier without me knowing. I just stood there shocked and said, "It's a piano." I later learned that my dad felt impressed that it was really important that I have that piano at that time of my life. My parents used a part of a small inheritance my mom received to purchase it.

That digital piano was moved into my bedroom Christmas morning and I played it into the wee hours of the night with headphones on. In the next few years, hundreds of improvisations happened on that digital piano and I wrote many songs. Because of the present of music from my grandparents and parents, those two pianos paved the foundation for a successful music career. I've written hundreds of songs that have been published digitally and in piano books, selling nearly 100,000 copies, and I have albums that have been streamed more than 100 million times.

The sacrifice that was made to give a piano to a teenager, who previously didn't want to practice and had quit piano, will forever be remembered as my best Christmas memory.

We never know how one act of kindness or sacrifice might lead to bigger things.

Jason Tonioli | www.tonioli.com

Chapter Twenty-Two

Grateful for Gratitude

We are commanded, my friends, to live in thanksgiving daily, always returning thanks for whatsoever we receive.

Why? Does God need our gratitude? No, we do.

I will never forget the Christmas of 2006. Shaina wanted a keyboard for Christmas.

I mean she really wanted a keyboard! We looked at used ones, but the cost was too much. Every chance she got though, Shaina would play one and just dream. As young ones often do, she pestered us incessantly about wanting a keyboard.

Finally, I sat her down and explained, "We just can't afford it." But then I said, "Be patient though, my dear, and I promise I'll get you one. All good things come to those who wait."

She never said another word about it, but we knew she was mightily disappointed. Then, for some reason, we felt as though we should make the sacrifice and get it for her. We did.

So, on Christmas morning, we opened our presents, but the keyboard was hidden away. Shaina seemed content and happy with what she'd received, and I noticed that.

Then when all the presents were opened, Mom led the family into the laundry room. There was the prized drum set for Hannah, the guitar for Travis and Sherise, and the keyboard for Shaina.

Hannah screamed and danced through the house. Travis and Sherise picked up the guitar and began to "plink." But Shaina–she took one look at the keyboard, screamed with excitement, and then turned and buried her face in my chest, and just held on to me. At first, I thought she was laughing. Then I realized she was crying–not just crying, she was sobbing with joy. For a long moment, she just held onto me and cried, and cried, and cried. No one noticed, but Dad was crying, too, as I do every time I think about that moment. I'm not sure there's anything a father appreciates more than a truly grateful child. Her tears of gratitude were more than ample payment for our sacrifice.

"... God so loved the world, that he gave his only begotten Son ..." (John 3:16).

Just imagine the joy the Father and the Son will share with us when we, with true understanding, fall at their feet, and bathe those feet with tears of joy and gratitude. That child who seeks to understand what has been done for them, and never stops expressing it, is the child that a parent loves to bless.

So, practice your gratitude like Shaina practiced piano. It is music to our Father and is the mark of a cultivated mind. To perfect gratitude is to master the natural man, and to know God.

Chapter Twenty-Three

A Savior

Christmas is a season for gifts.

May I speak of the greatest single gift that has ever been given?

Consider these words: "For God so loved the world, that he gave his only begotten Son, that whosoever believeth in him should not perish, but have everlasting life" (John 3:16). What a gift!

On the night those shepherds, just and holy men they were, kept watch over their flock by night, an angel of the Lord appeared in glory to them and announced, "For unto you is born this day in the city of David a Saviour, which is Christ the Lord" (Luke 2:11) —a Savior, the gift of a Savior.

You know, for most of my life, I have not fully appreciated this title of the Master. Maybe I still don't. But I know that my understanding has changed. May I share an experience?

Years ago, while at the hospital for the birth of one of our children, things had progressed to that point where delivery of the child was only moments away. I was as tense as a cat. I watched the monitoring nurse doing routine checks, and noticed suddenly her facial expression changed. I sensed instantly that something was wrong.

A call went out, a doctor ran into the room, and confirmed that the baby was in serious trouble. Normal delivery would kill her. Even though it was an unlikely time of the day, the call went throughout the hospital, and a team of doctors and nurses was scrambled. All the while, one doctor and one nurse worked with great effort and skill to save my baby's life. Within minutes of the first alarm, an emergency cesarean section was performed and the baby was saved.

The nurses took me and the baby down to the nursery where she was cleaned and examined. When they were done, I had the choice privilege of holding her for the first time. As I sat in that chair and looked into that little face, I was overcome with one of the most profound feelings of gratitude I have ever felt in my life, gratitude to my dear wife for her sacrifice, gratitude to God for a beloved and perfect new daughter, and not the least, gratitude to trained, self-sacrificing doctors and nurses, saviors if you will of my little daughter.

Now every so often, I look at her and remember how I almost lost her, and how she was saved from sure death. Then I'm reminded in a deeper and a more personal way of what it means to have the gift of a Savior, which is Christ the Lord.

PART 2

"And so it was, that, while they were there, the days were accomplished that she should be delivered. And she brought forth her firstborn son, and wrapped him in swaddling clothes, and laid him in a manger; because there was no room for them in the inn" (Luke 2:6-7).

Chapter Twenty-Four

The Christmas Story

"And it came to pass in those days, that there went out a decree from Caesar Augustus, that all the world should be taxed. And this taxing was first made when Cyrenius was governor of Syria. And all went to be taxed, every one into his own city. And Joseph also went up from Galilee, out of the city of Nazareth into Judaea, unto the city of David, which is called Bethlehem; (because he was of the house and lineage of David:) To be taxed with Mary, his espoused wife, being great with child" (Luke 2:1-5).

"And so it was, that, while they were there, the days were accomplished that she should be delivered. And she brought forth her firstborn son, and wrapped him in swaddling clothes, and laid him in a manger; because there was no room for them in the inn" (Luke 2:6-7).

"And there were in the same country shepherds abiding in the field, keeping watch over their flock by night. And, lo, the angel of the Lord came upon them, and the glory of the Lord shone round about them: and they were sore afraid." (Luke 2:8-9)

"And the angel said unto them, Fear not: for, behold, I bring you good tidings of great joy, which shall be to all people. For unto you is born this day in the city of David a Saviour, which is Christ the Lord." (Luke 2:10-11).

"And this shall be a sign unto you; Ye [You] shall find the babe wrapped in swaddling clothes, lying in a manger. And suddenly there was with the angel a multitude of the heavenly host praising God, and saying, Glory to God in the highest, and on earth peace, good will toward men" (Luke 2:12-14).

"And it came to pass, as the angels were gone away from them into heaven, the shepherds said one to another, Let us now go even unto Bethlehem, and see this thing which is come to pass, which the Lord hath made known unto us. And they came with haste, and found Mary, and Joseph, and the babe lying in a manger. " (Luke 2:15-16).

"And when they had seen it, they made known abroad the saying, which was told them concerning this child. And all they that heard it wondered at those things which were told them by the shepherds." (Luke 2:17-18).

"But Mary kept all these things, and pondered them in her heart. And the shepherds returned, glorifying and praising God for all the things that they had heard and seen, as it was told unto them." (Luke 2:19-20).

I want you to know, this story is true.

Merry Christmas to you.

Sources:

From Luke 2

Chapter Twenty-Five

Ahaz's Sign

The story of Christmas began long before those events in Bethlehem. Holy men and women of God looked forward to the birth of the Lord Jesus Christ, virtually from the dawn of creation. This is that story.

More than 700 years before the birth of the Savior, the people of Jerusalem were frightened. Their peace was threatened by a ruthless power from the north, called Assyria, who was taking over country after country. Judah's neighbors, Ephraim and Syria, were hastily forming political alliances to guard against the threat.

Judah's king, Ahaz, refused to join the alliance, choosing instead to bargain with Assyria directly for his nation's safety. The Kings of Ephraim and Syria were angered that Ahaz and Judah would not join them and promised to invade and remove Ahaz as King. Isaiah the prophet came to Ahaz and told him not to fear the two allied kings. Don't listen to them, be at peace, and trust the Lord. But the imminent political threat was too much for the wicked Ahaz. In his heart, he would not believe it. How could he? Their doom seemed sure, in spite of Isaiah's promises. Knowing that, Isaiah said, "Ask thee a sign of the Lord thy God; ask it either in the depth, or in the height above" (Isaiah 7:11). To seek signs of ourselves is evil, but when the Lord commands us to ask for one, it is evil not to. Moreover, to be told that his sign can come from the depths of hell or the heights of heaven, whatever he wants, must mean that God was very determined that this doubting man believed His promises.

Stubbornly, Ahaz refused to ask. Isaiah was disgusted with him and all his nation and said the Lord would give him a sign anyway. "Behold," He said, addressing himself now to all the nation, "a virgin shall conceive, and bear a son, and shall call His name Immanuel" (Isaiah 7:14). Immanuel means God with us. How could a virgin bear a son?

That's impossible. Yet, God did the impossible on that first Christmas when Jesus was born. But, Ahaz would not live to see the sign fulfilled.

Christ would not be born for another seven hundred years. So, why was it given? This was not just a sign to Ahaz, but to all the children of God that doubt Him and His promises. Every Christmas is a reminder that God did once, and can do again, the impossible.

Any of you that are troubled for any reason and seek peace, need only look at the miracle of Christmas to awaken your latent faith.

This is, ironically, the season of the coldest weather in the northern hemisphere and yet for a time, the warmest hearts. When Christmas comes "God is with us" again, in our hearts, our homes, and even our music. One need only look at how our world changes this time of year to know that Christ is still in Christmas.

Indeed, Christmas is an everlasting sign to a doubting world that God is still with us, that He loves us, and that He can still do the impossible, this time for you and me.

Chapter Twenty-Six

Mary, Mother of Jesus

Mary was of the royal house of God. She was a princess by birth. She was a woman of prophecy. Her identity, mission, and name were known hundreds of years before she was born. She was more beautiful and fair than any woman of her day. She was of sufficient spiritual capacity to be transfigured and stand in the presence of God and angels.

She was favored above all women, of all time. It was she who was selected above all women to be the mother of God's only Begotten Son. Of sufficient stature was she that when Gabriel came to her, he did obeisance to her and Mary wondered why an angel would salute her so.

She was chosen to be the mother of the greatest man who would ever live. He was born to be the greatest King in this world's history and she was chosen to help Him. She was chosen to have a relationship with the God of Heaven, different from any other. When she said, "Be it unto me according to thy word" (Luke 1:38), Mary accepted a responsibility and burden, like no woman has ever known.

What a trial it must have been for this chaste and modest young woman to have anyone think of her as an adulteress. In an ecstasy of spirit with Elizabeth, Mary praised the Lord with a profundity and power that has few equals in scripture.

Meekly, Mary bore the difficult journey to Bethlehem when her time was full. There is no scriptural record that this remarkable woman ever weakened or complained of all that she was called to bear. Some mothers tend to overprotect, but not Mary. She understood from the beginning that this child was for the world. When the shepherds came in from the field, she let them see Him.

From the beginning and throughout her life, she sacrificed her name, reputation, will, wants, and personal comfort for her son. It is a law of God that commensurate with great blessings are great trials. I believe Mary was tried in mortality as no other woman has ever been. In the temple, Simeon promised her that her Son would be the subject of persecution and would one day meet the point of a sword; yet there is no evidence that she shrank back from the challenge of standing by Him throughout His life. She was true to Him until death.

After all that Mary had witnessed of the miraculous, it speaks to her spiritual maturity that she kept sacred secrets, and could thus be trusted by God. Mary was obedient, a woman of the law. Though her Son would fulfill the Law of Moses, yet she still complied with it. Though Mary had been the woman on whom God had bestowed such infinite favor, yet she was faithful and obedient to the leadership of her beloved husband Joseph. She followed him in flight into Egypt and eventually to Nazareth, where they settled.

In the spirit of worship, she came up to Jerusalem every year for the feast of the Passover. On one of these trips, she and Joseph lost Jesus for several days. Can you imagine how it must have anguished her when they couldn't find Him? "Oh my, we lost the Son of God."

Mary bore several more children. At the marriage in Cana, she presided over the festivities, and when they ran out of wine, she demonstrated an implicit faith in her perfect Son. It is worthy to note the tender and loving relationship between Mary and her Son. Contrary to what appears in some scriptural texts, He was never unkind, dismissive, or disrespectful of her. She was of queenly nobility to Him. In terrible pain, she was at His bleeding feet when He hung on the cross, and resigned herself into the care of John the Beloved at her Son's request.

But, where was Joseph? Could it be that with all that she has borne, now too, she is a widow? We know very little that we can trust in her last years, but we know enough of the first 50 years of her life to declare with certainty that the trust placed in her by a loving Heavenly Father was deserved. Mary was called and foreordained from before the world's creation. Of all our Father's daughters, she stands supreme as the most faithful and powerful of them all. Someday we will more fully know how noble and great she really was. She was and is a holy woman of God!

Chapter Twenty-Seven

The Annunciation to Mary

Knowing that we mortals tend to resist change, our Father in Heaven wisely prepares us before critical decisions are to be made by schooling our feelings and informing our agency. In that light, consider what happened to Mary, the Mother of Jesus.

"And in the sixth month the angel Gabriel was sent from God unto a city of Galilee named Nazareth" (Luke 1:26). He was sent "to a virgin espoused to a man whose name was Joseph, of the House of David, and the virgin's name was Mary" (Luke 1:27). By merciful providence, Mary was not to be alone to bear God's Son. Joseph, of kingly descent, was Mary's chosen companion and protector.

The angel "came in unto her, and said, Hail, thou that art highly favored. The Lord is with thee, blessed art thou among women" (Luke 1:28). Mary stands preeminent— chosen and blessed because of her faith. Rightly, her name means "exalted." To our Father in Heaven, she is precious.

"And when she saw him, she was troubled at his saying and cast in her mind what manner of salutation this should be" (Luke 1:29). The sight of the angel frightened and confused her. Why was he greeting her with such reverence?

"Fear not, Mary: for thou hast found favor with God. And thou shalt conceive in thy womb and bring forth a son and shalt call his name Jesus" (Luke 1:30-31). Motherhood is the highest, holiest calling on earth, but to be the mother of Jesus the Christ, He would be as He was named. His name means Savior.

"He shall be great, and shall be called the Son of the Highest: and the Lord God shall give unto Him the throne of His Father David, and He shall reign over the house of Israel forever, and of His kingdom, there shall be no end" (Luke 1:32-33). This promise must have stayed with her for the rest of her life. No matter the mortal realities, her Son was a Prince—the Prince of Peace, worlds without end. No son ever brought more honor and glory to his mother than did Jesus.

But to have a son and be not married—"How shall this be," Mary said, "seeing I know not a man" (Luke 1:34). Mary did not as yet comprehend who and what her Son was to be.

"The Holy Ghost shall come upon thee," Gabriel taught, "and the power of the Highest shall overshadow thee, therefore also that holy thing that shall be born of thee shall be called the Son of God" (Luke 1:35). This Son was to be like no other before or after—He was the only Son God ever sired into mortality—the Only Begotten in the flesh. The Son of God Himself was coming to earth and she was to prepare His physical tabernacle and be His Mother.

And then as if to further confirm her overwhelmed faith— "And thy cousin Elizabeth, she hath also conceived a son in her old age, and this is the sixth month with her who was called barren. For with God nothing shall be impossible" (Luke 1:36-37). When all the powers of hell would be let loose on Mary and her family, she would always remember and know—God can do the impossible. What serenity and peace this proven truth must have been to her!

The call was explained and extended, her calling and election in mortality was offered. Now…"Behold, the handmaid of the Lord," Mary said in meek submission, "Be it unto me according to thy word" (Luke 1:38). Notably, before Jesus would say, "Not my will but thine be done" (Luke 22:42), His Mother, in principle, would say it first.

Besides her Son, did any mortal ever accept so much with so few words? My soul overflows with reverence and awe for Mary—what manner of woman was she, and how did heaven consider her? I can't even find the words.

Bethlehem and John the Baptist

Have you ever noticed how often we tell the story of Christmas and skip over the birth of John the Baptist? I don't think we should. To neglect John in telling that story is like neglecting your preparations for Christmas until the morning of.

Before there was John the Baptist, there was John the baby.

Before Matthew, Mark, Luke, and John wrote of Jesus, John the Baptist kept a record first. As in his life, John pointed people to Jesus, so too did he in his birth.

Before Gabriel came to Mary, he appeared to an old man named Zacharias in the Temple. "Fear not, Zacharias," he said, "thy prayer is heard; and thy wife Elizabeth shall bear thee a son, and thou shalt call his name John" (Luke 1:13). The angel promised that this little boy would bring much joy to many people, but not just because he was a baby, but because he would "be great in the sight of the Lord.... Many of the children of Israel shall he turn to the Lord their God" (Luke 1:15-16). John would go before the Savior and "...make ready a people prepared for the Lord" (Luke 1:17).

Zacharias struggled to believe what he was hearing. I don't blame him! Elizabeth was an older woman. Nonetheless, Mary's miraculous conception was not the first. Before Mary went into hiding with a child she couldn't explain, Elizabeth was there.

One day, a beautiful young woman, sent by an angel, came into the courtyard of Elizabeth's home and called out a greeting. In the womb, John leaped for joy, and he and his mother were filled with the Holy Ghost. It is sublime that at that moment John bore witness of the Messiah before he even had a voice. The two sons of prophecy and their sainted mothers spent the next three months together.

As John prepared the way for Jesus, so Elizabeth prepared and consoled Mary. Before the people heard the shepherds' witness of a coming Messiah, they were astonished at the new voice and testimony of Zacharias.

His prophecies resonated through the hills and hearts of the Jews, filling them with grand expectations. Then and later, all who ever knew John couldn't wait to meet Jesus.

On the night of the Savior's birth in Bethlehem, John was three months old in Hebron. Knowing what Elizabeth knew of Mary and the bond they shared, I wonder how far away she really was from her young cousin.

When Herod's soldiers came, you know they were looking for two famous babies—not one.

While the angel sent Joseph and Mary into Egypt to save Jesus, Zacharias sent John and Elizabeth into the wilderness. Joseph and Jesus escaped, but the soldiers killed Zacharias. He would not give up his son. As Jesus grew up with his Father, hewing wood, so John grew up in the wilderness, eating locusts and wild honey. As Jesus waited and prepared to bring men to His Father, so John waited and prepared to bring men to Jesus.

Luke's story of Christmas tells of a special babe whose birth pointed men to Jesus' birth and John was born to prepare the way for Him. God grant that we be like John, that in all that we are, all that we say, all that we do, men want to learn of Christ.

Chapter Twenty-Nine

Joseph

You know, as a baby, the Lord Jesus was as weak and vulnerable as any other child ever born. And so in the wisdom of God, a man was chosen as a protector of the Christ Child and His mother. That man was Joseph, the carpenter.

There's a principle that says, "Where much is given, much is required." Joseph was blessed with the love and the hand of the most beautiful maiden in all the land.

Mary was a precious and chosen young woman. Yet, he was also entrusted to protect her and guide the development of God's only Begotten Son. It was not a small trust.

Now, consider the following the next time you read the story about Joseph.

Obedient to the angel, Joseph married Mary and named her child Jesus. What if Joseph had been an extremist and decided to have her stoned as an adulteress? Obedient to the law, Joseph returned to Bethlehem to be taxed with Mary, his wife, and thus he fulfilled the prophecy. What if he'd refused, and the trip was never made?

Devotedly, upon arriving in Bethlehem, Joseph sought the best for Mary in the delivery of her child, going to numerous inns. But since no one would make room for them, at least he found a stable—and faithfully, Joseph brought Jesus and Mary to the Temple to do for them, after the Savior's birth, according to the requirements of the Law of Moses. It was there that Simeon and Anna met them, and thus fulfilled God's promise to the aged Simeon. What if Joseph had never come?

And the wise men—humbly and appreciatively, Joseph accepted the gifts offered by them. What if he had been too proud to take charity? What then?

Just imagine how the course of history would have been altered if Joseph had been slow to wake up, and slow to obey when the angel came and warned him of the approach of Herod's murderous soldiers?

Joseph was submissive to God. He fled into a strange land, taking Mary and the baby, and remained there until the angel bid him return.

True to his role, through the Savior's boyhood, Joseph taught Jesus the trade of a carpenter and loved Him deeply enough to seek Him, sorrowing for many days when He disappeared in Jerusalem at the age of twelve.

Now consider this: When the Savior hung upon the cross at the end of His life, He committed the care of His beloved mother into the hands of John the Beloved, one of the apostles. So, where was Joseph? Well, we don't know for sure. Maybe it was the death of Joseph that perfected the Savior's empathy sufficient to bring Him to tears at the death of His friend, Lazarus, or moved Him to restore the life of the daughter of Jairus and the son of the widow of Nain, and enables Him now to comfort us when we lose those that we love. He understands perfectly.

Isaiah spoke of the Savior as "… a man of sorrows, and acquainted with grief…" (Isaiah 53:3). Surely Joseph, who loved Him, could no more have escaped the pain that his son suffered than a parent who sees his child suffer now.

Joseph, the carpenter, blessed not only the lives of Jesus and Mary with his faith and devotion, but indeed, all of history. Thanks be to God for the man Joseph and the gifts he gave. May we all live and return such gifts to the Savior now.

Chapter Thirty

The Birth

I want to tell a familiar story with this in mind: Christmas is all about love.

"And it came to pass in those days, that there went out a decree from Caesar Augustus, that all the world should be taxed " (Luke 2:1).

You know, as Caesar and the oppressive Roman Empire counted and taxed the goods of life from its subjects, ("And this taxing was first made when Cyrenius was governor of Syria", (Luke 2:2), at the same time, a true king was born who would also number His sheep, but would free them and give them the abundance of life—not take it.

Sometimes I wonder why that's in there. The book of Luke was a letter written to a friend. This parenthetical comment was directed by Luke to his friend Theophilus, to give him a point of time reference for the beginning of his story.

Another thought is that every year we send Christmas cards with expressions of love, faith, and greeting. So, what does that make the Book of Luke then?—the world's first Christmas card?

"And all went to be taxed, every one unto his own city. And Joseph also went up from Galilee, out of the city of Nazareth, into Judaea, unto the city of David, which is called Bethlehem; (because he was of the house and lineage of David) To be taxed with Mary, his espoused wife, being great with child" (Luke 2:3-5).

No matter what the customs of the Jews, Joseph and Mary returned to Bethlehem because God wanted them to, because Jesus had to be born in Bethlehem to fulfill the words of the prophets. We can only imagine how arduous that journey must have been for Mary, who was almost ready to have the baby. Yet sacrifice, then and now, brings forth the blessings of heaven.

"And so it was, that, while they were there, the days were accomplished that she should be delivered. And she brought forth her firstborn son,..." (Luke 2:6-7).

Jesus was Mary's firstborn, and the birthright son of Joseph's family. Later, Mary would have at least four more sons and at least two daughters. So I guess you could say in more ways than one, Jesus stood at the head of a large family.

"... and wrapped him in swaddling clothes,..." (Luke 2:7).

To swaddle was to wrap the newborn to provide comfort and security. Isaiah prophesied in the Old Testament that a virgin would conceive and bring forth a son, and then he said right after that, that "...Butter and honey shall he eat..." (Isaiah 7:12-15), meaning the son of the virgin. Butter and honey were staples in the diet of the poor. The meaning seems to be that Jesus would be born in poverty.

"... and laid him in a manger; because there was no room for them in the inn[s]" (Luke 2:7).

Mary's condition would have been obvious. Imagine if an expectant mother came to your door. Could you ever turn her away? Yet in the hardness of their hearts, no one would make room for her in the inns.

Descended from the royal courts on high, the Prince of Peace, the King of Heaven, was born in His own city, among His own people, in a stable. Bethlehem marked the beginning of the journey for the Savior, who would descend below all things that He might rise above all things.

My friends, I hope with all of my heart that the love of the Savior fills your heart this Christmas, and that love spreads to all men as you make room for Him.

Merry Christmas.

Chapter Thirty-One

Swaddling Clothes

I have often pondered how Mary felt about the circumstances surrounding the birth of Jesus. There is no doubt in my mind that she and Joseph desired to give the very best care they could to this special baby. The well-known Christmas story found in Luke 2 tells of Mary putting her newborn son in "swaddling clothes".

"And she brought forth her firstborn son, and wrapped him in swaddling clothes, and laid him in a manger; because there was no room for them in the inn." (Luke 2:7)

I have read some authors' explanations of swaddling clothes as mere rags which were wrapped around the babe, due to a lack of financial resources which Joseph and Mary had. That description does not ring true to me.

So, what were swaddling clothes during that time period and why was it so significant for Luke to mention infant care twice in the same chapter? We were not there to provide a first-hand account of what happened, but Christian and Hebrew scholars have suggested possible reasons and symbolism attached to this practice.

According to ancient Greek and Jewish sources, wrapping an infant in this way would be usual, expected, and meaningful. It was practiced by rich and poor alike. As far back as the sixth century B.C. during the time of the prophet Ezekiel, and referred to in Ezekiel 16:4, swaddling was a sign that an infant was properly cared for. At the time Christ was born, the Jewish infants would have the umbilical cord cut, washed, and then rubbed with a small amount of powdered salt for drying and cleansing. In ancient Jewish culture, salt signified that the parents would raise the child to be truthful and faithful. The baby was then wrapped, or swaddled. There are several theories as to the type of fabric and size of the cloth used – but often suggesting there were several yards of fabric strips or larger pieces similar to a small blanket.

Early Christian tradition had Mary spinning so that she would have good cloth and thread to make bands of swaddling cloth. Some scholars think that swaddling bands were embroidered with symbols, indicating family history and genealogy. Symbols were exactly the same on both sides, signifying that the outward and inward life were the same, and there was no wrong side to their character. On the wedding day, standing under a canopy, these adorned bands would be tied around the clasped right hands of the bride and groom. These bands would later be used to fasten the swaddling clothes of their own children. I like to imagine Mary using these bands, which she had lovingly prepared, to help the child feel comfortable and secure the "swaddling clothes" to the child. These were far from a description of "rags".

Not too far from the stable where the holy family rested, there were others who had experience using swaddling bands. They were shepherds watching their flocks. However, it is likely that they were not ordinary shepherds. Tradition suggests that in that area there were Levitical shepherds who were tasked with raising the sacrifices which would be offered in the temple. When a first-born lamb was born, it was taken to a shelter and placed in a manger. Then the shepherd would swaddle the lamb because the sacrifice had to be without spot or blemish.

On the sacred night that Jesus came into the world, an angel announced to nearby shepherds that a "Saviour, Christ the Lord" was born and said,

"And this shall be a sign unto you; Ye shall find the babe wrapped in swaddling clothes, lying in a manger." (Luke 2:12)

The shepherds "came with haste and found Mary, and Joseph, and the babe lying in a manger" (Luke 2:16). Seeing a child in swaddling clothes was expected, but to be lying in a manger, just as their sacrificial lambs, would not go unnoticed. A baby was born in the same place as the Passover lambs were born, swaddled like a Passover lamb, and pointing to the fact that the Messiah was the Lamb of God.

The Wise Men

A wise man is one who has knowledge and understands how best to use it. There is nothing more wise than to find and then follow the Lord Jesus Christ.

After Jesus was born, "...there came wise men from the east to Jerusalem, saying, Where is he that is born King of the Jews? For we have seen His star in the east, and are come to worship Him" (Matthew 2:1-2).

The Bible foretells nothing of a new star, yet somehow these faithful disciples knew it was coming, and when it appeared they understood it to be the sign of the Messiah. Like all the faithful, they wanted to see Him, be with Him—worship Him. And so, they set out to find Him.

Because light always stirs up darkness, Herod and "all Jerusalem" was "troubled" at the news of the child. Herod "greatly feared" Him as the deliverer spoken of by the prophets, even though He refused to believe and obey. He demanded of the Jews to know where Christ would be born. He was told Bethlehem. Then Herod "called the wise men privily," and learned that the star had appeared almost two years before.

He feigned faith, but his intent was to use the Wise Men to find Jesus and kill Him. So he sent them on to Bethlehem, saying, "Go and search diligently for the young child; and when ye have found him, bring me word again that I may come and worship Him also" (Matthew 2:8).

As the Wise Men began the short journey to Bethlehem, the star that had begun their long journey in the east reappeared, and beckoned them to follow.

"They rejoiced with exceedingly great joy" to see it again. It "...went before them until it came and stood over where the young child was" (Matthew 2:9).

That star was for them as Christ is for us, a heavenly light so far away, and yet so close and personal. "And when they came into the house, they saw the young child with Mary, His mother, and fell down and worshipped Him..." (Matthew 2:11).

This is why they were called Wise Men. Jesus had "no form nor comeliness, " and "no beauty that we should desire Him." These grown and wise, seasoned and mature men fell to their knees before him in reverence and meek adoration. They were truly wise for they knew of Him what man cannot know without revelation. This child was their Savior and Redeemer.

"...When they had opened their treasures, they presented Him gifts; gold, and frankincense, and myrrh" (Matthew 2:11), because those who love the Lord give Him all that they have as well as all that they are.

As the Wise Men settled down to sleep that night, they were "warned of God in a dream not to return to Herod." They rose and departed the country another way. An angel of the Lord then appeared to Joseph in a dream saying, "Arise, and take the young child and His mother and flee into Egypt... for Herod will seek the young child to destroy Him'" (Matthew 2:13). The danger was real. Isaiah said Jesus "... would grow up before Him as a tender plant" (Isaiah 53:2).

As a child, Jesus was as subject to cold, hunger, and to death as any other child. When warned of impending danger, immediately Joseph arose and took Jesus and His mother by night and fled into Egypt. Herod was incensed at being so deceived and in an effort to kill the Son of God, he "... sent forth and slew all the children in Bethlehem and in all the coasts thereof from two years old and under..." (Matthew 2:16).

This was the most foolish thing any man could have ever done.

This story is about wise and foolish men.

Fools still ignore and scorn the Son of God.

The wise still seek Him.

If you would be wise in the wisest of all wisdom, "...Ask and it shall be given you; seek, and ye shall find; knock, and it shall be opened unto you" (Matthew 7:7). Remember, just as it was that night for the Wise Men, so will it be for you—the door is still open.

Chapter Thirty-Three

The Babe of Bethlehem

Jesus, the Babe of Bethlehem — He lived, and today He lives again and watches over us as Mary once watched over Him. Where once He was cradled as a helpless babe in a lowly manger, now He reigns as King of Kings and Lord of Lords in courts of eternal glory.

He was once tender and fragile, helpless, as susceptible to death and injury as any other, but now He is all-powerful and all-wise, the author and finisher of our faith.

He is the light and the life of the world. Where this world was dark and cruel on the night He came, He will make it glorious and perfect.

He came as a babe, but He was God, sent to a world that had forgotten God. And through Him, all may be one with God.

Like every other baby ever born, His memory was veiled and His innocence sweet. He descended from a heavenly throne and never stopped that plunging descent until he was raised upon the cross. But now, He stands above us all with hands outstretched, inviting us to be one with Him where He is. He was comprehended by none, but now He comprehends and loves us all.

Be assured that as angels announced with heart and voice His coming once, they will do so again. Shepherds were His witnesses then, and they still are. He came once as a suffering servant. He will come again, this time a conquering King.

At His birth, He was adored by few, hated by some, and ignored by most—but no one can ignore Him now. He is our Savior and Redeemer, meriting our worship, and universal adoration.

He was born a subject of Rome, a slave to Caesar's whim, but He rose as the King to conquer all, even death and hell.

Mary, His mother, loved Him, and from Bethlehem to Calvary she never left Him. Mary wrapped Him in swaddling clothes when He was born, but now, those swaddling clothes are the resplendent white robes of eternal glory.

At His first coming, only Mary and Joseph saw to His comfort and care. The world turned a cold heart. But we have His promise—when He comes again, His heart will be turned to those who have waited long for Him. They will come forth, His loving kindness burning in their heart's memory forever.

As Joseph and Mary took Him to Egypt and saved him from Herod's hate and man's envy, so too, He will take us out of Egypt—the world, to another world where hate and envy ne'er annoy.

He was born to a stable and raised to mansions of glory. On that first Christmas night, no one understood and so no one made room for Him—but now, His heart, broad as the heavens, swells wide as eternity. There is, thank God, room for us all.

Chapter Thirty-Four

Simeon and Anna

I have heard it said recently, if all you know is what you see with your natural eyes and hear with your natural ears, then you will not know very much. Those who live by the Holy Ghost see, hear, and know much more than those of the world can enjoy, as this Christmas story illustrates.

Forty days after the Savior's birth, Joseph and Mary brought him to the Temple in Jerusalem. Since the Passover, every firstborn son in Israel belonged to the Lord. Joseph and Mary made an offering in their poverty of two turtledoves to redeem him. To see it another way, Joseph made a sacrificial offering to redeem his son, just as Heavenly Father would later make a sacrificial offering of His Son and redeem all mankind.

"And, behold, there was a man in Jerusalem, whose name was Simeon; and the same man was just and devout, waiting for the consolation of Israel: and the Holy Ghost was upon him. And it was revealed unto him by the Holy Ghost that he should not see death, before he had seen the Lord's Christ" (Luke 2:25-26).

On that day, and at that time, the Spirit led Simeon into the crowded temple just as Joseph and Mary arrived there. With all of Jerusalem as an audience, the Holy Ghost identified Jesus to Simeon. He came and took the blessed infant in his arms. "Lord," he said in humble praise, "now lettest thou thy servant depart in peace, according to the word: For mine eyes have seen thy salvation, which thou hast prepared before the face of all people; a light to lighten the Gentiles and the glory of thy people Israel" (Luke 2:29-31).

Simeon was joyously happy because that day which he had lived for, for so long, had come. Joseph and Mary "... marvelled at those things which were spoken of him" (Luke 2:33). Seldom does the Lord reveal all His word at once. Line upon line, revelation comes incrementally and in packets to the faithful. Joseph and Mary were still learning who their Son really was.

Then, Simeon turned to Mary and spoke to her sensitive soul. "This child," he said, as if in "warning," "is set for the fall and rising again of many in Israel; and for a sign which shall be spoken against" (Luke 2:34). Your Son, Mary, will reveal the hearts of all men. He will be both loved and hated. His name will be had for good and evil among all men. Those who love light and truth will come in reverence to Him and will rise with him. Those who love darkness rather than light will be exposed, and they will hate Him and they will fall. "Yea," he continued, as if in prophetic illustration, "Yea, a sword shall pierce through thy own soul also, that the thoughts of many hearts may be revealed" (Luke 2:35).

There was another witness of Christ that day in the temple. "And there was one Anna, a prophetess…of the tribe of Aser; she was of great age… [and] was a widow of about fourscore and four years, which departed not from the temple, but served God with fastings and prayers night and day. And she coming in that instant gave thanks likewise unto the Lord, and spake of him to all them that looked for redemption in Jerusalem" (Luke 2:36-38).

Anna, the prophetess, was inspired to know that the baby was Jesus Christ and shared this with others. However, Simeon's words were not as comforting. What kind of statement is that to make to a mother in the joy of a new son? No wonder people ignore this part of the Christmas story. But, this prophecy embodies the real meaning of Christmas and the Savior's life. You see, it is life at the other end of the manger that gives this moment of nativity in Bethlehem its ultimate meaning.

Gethsemane, Golgotha, and the Garden Tomb give Christmas its real meaning and joy, and the old man about to die, Simeon, and Anna who came moments later, knew that. All of us have and will fall, but praise God from whom all blessings flow—joy to the world, indeed, for we can rise again.

When we see Christmas as Simeon did, the season becomes one of worship, and the joy and peace last all year. The best gifts become those that express the most love for God and man.

Chapter Thirty-Five

Boyhood of Jesus

The Lord Jesus Christ was the one perfect being this world has ever known. When He said "follow me," it was not just in where He went, but in the way He went. From His childhood, He was the perfect example.

An angel of the Lord appeared to Joseph in Egypt and told him that it was safe to take Mary and Jesus back to Israel. It was his intention to return to Bethlehem, but when he learned that Herod's son ruled there, he feared going back. Directed again by the angel, he went to an obscure Galilean village called Nazareth (Matthew 2:19-23).

 And there, Jesus grew up with his brethren. He was the oldest of five brothers, James, Joses, Simon and Judas, and at least two sisters (Matthew 13:55-56).

At the age of twelve, Jesus traveled with His parents to Jerusalem for the feast of the Passover. When they set out for home, Jesus stayed back. Three days later, they found Him in the Temple, teaching the doctors and answering their questions. It was an amazing spectacle, both to His audience and His parents, to see this mere boy teaching the gospel to the wisest of His day.

"Son," His mother said, "why hast thou thus dealt with us? Behold thy father and I have sought thee sorrowing" (Luke 2:48).

"How is it that ye sought me," he said, "wist ye not that I must be about my father's business?" (Luke 2:49). He had tarried by design to teach and bring souls unto God. Where else should his parents have looked for Him than in the Temple—His Father's house.

Nevertheless, He obeyed His parents and went home with them. By the age of twelve, Jesus knew He was God's son, not Joseph's son. However, Jesus was born with no memory of his former glory. Like every other child, He grew line upon line and precept upon precept, increasing in wisdom, except, He grew until no man on earth was wise enough to teach Him. And yet, as He grew powerful, He also increased in favor with God and man (Luke 2:52).

He always did those things that pleased His Heavenly Father, and consequently, the grace of God was upon Him (Luke 2:40), and never left Him. Similarly, He understood love and by that power men loved Him.

Jesus knew who He was and what He was born to do, and yet for 30 years, He was the carpenter's son, working under Joseph, all the while waiting—preparing, growing in strength, wisdom, and spirituality. When it was time, he came out of Galilee to Jordan, unto John, to be baptized, having prepared Himself spiritually, intellectually, physically, and socially, just as we must do if we would go where He went, and become as He was.

Chapter Thirty-Six

Christmas and the Golden Rule

Two millennia ago, angels sang out in heavenly triumph, "Glory to God in the highest, and on earth peace, good will toward men" (Luke 2:14). The Savior is still the Prince of Peace. So, why is there so little good will now?

Why in our day do we live with wars and rumors of war? Why do we have pestilence and plagues approaching epidemic proportions? Explain to me, if you please, the logic of weapons of mass destruction. Why? Terrorists, why do we have them and their twisted minds?

Why is it that people will be decimated by disease and starvation? Why do earthquakes, volcanoes, hurricanes, fires, floods, and other disasters increase and ruin lives and property? Why is it that there are those who ruin the land for greed?

What has happened to us? Has our world gone crazy? Why is there so much anger and hate? Why are there so many people so unhappy and so much heartbreak and abuse in homes? It is because we have not understood!

There is a doctrine of the Prince of Peace so little considered, but so powerful in scope that if applied would literally change our world. Other than His Atonement, there is perhaps no other teaching so closely connected with the Lord's ministry. The awesome power to change our lives, our families, and our world lies in a simple formula.

He said, "...all things whatsoever ye would that men should do to you, do ye even so to them..." (Matthew 7:12). As the love of men waxes cold, think of the global warming of hearts that would come if all men treated each other as they would want to be treated? How should I treat my wife and children? I treat them like I would want them to treat me. To do this, I must place myself in their minds and hearts and then act.

I know that some will scoff and say that this is nothing more than words in the wind and that it's not practical. Please explain to me how war is practical. Where have threats, hate, envy, and greed ever made the world better? I'm not saying there's not a time to fight, but if we are going to fight, let's do it on the Lord's terms.

When an adulterous woman was thrown at Christ's feet to be condemned, He wouldn't. When others shunned publicans and harlots, He wouldn't. When the disciples wanted to send away a pleading Gentile woman, He wouldn't. While everyone else ran from a man possessed with a legion of devils, Jesus went to him and healed him. And, as for vengeance, when He suffered and bled in Gethsemane, He didn't come out of that bitter and resenting us, but loved us all the more.

He was beaten, mocked, spit upon, and pierced in His brow with thorns. His words were twisted and His garments were stripped from Him in public. Yet, with quiet dignity, He stood it, returning good for evil, love for hate. He did not give those who meant Him harm what they wanted, but gave them what they really needed. As the Romans crucified Him, He asked that they be forgiven.

The golden rule, not the rule of gold, was the rule of the Savior's life. Can anyone doubt that He changed the world for good? My friends, returning hate for hate only breeds more hate.

Where are you Christmas? Why have you gone away? Why can't we keep you all year long? We can!

The Spirit of Christmas is the Spirit of Christ. This year, don't lose it. Love thy neighbor as thyself is the law, and the golden rule is how we do it. This year, give the real gift of gold, the golden rule. Shake this world to its core. Start with your family, and let love become a global epidemic. It will work! I promise. Peace and good will will come. Merry Christmas, and God Bless us to follow His example.

Chapter Thirty-Seven

Christmas Symbolism

Nothing about the Christmas story, I want you to know, is accidental or haphazard. Every part of that beautifully simple story is a story in and of itself, and all of it bears witness to the living reality of our Savior.

For example: During the Savior's ministry, He was called the Bread of Life. Bread is now, as it was then, the staff of life. It's the mainstay of our diet. Jesus, the Bread of Life, was born in Bethlehem. Bethlehem means House of Bread.

Jesus is the Good Shepherd; and who was it that was privileged first to see Him and proclaim His birth? – Shepherds, those who tended the flocks.

Many scriptures refer to Jesus as the Lamb of God, He who was to die for our sins. Well, those flocks that were on the hills around Bethlehem that night – more than likely they were Temple Lambs destined for sacrifice for the sins of the people on the altars of the Temple.

How fitting it is that He was called the Bright and Morning Star by John the Baptist. It is fitting that as His sign, a new star, brighter than any other, appeared in the heavens.

And again, laid in a manger, a symbol of His lowliness, the Savior's beginnings were as humble and as lowly as any child that has ever been born. How appropriate it is then, that later He commanded us to become as children – meek, lowly, and humble.

Also, in the Christmas story, there are repeated references to David, that the Christ Child would be born David's son in David's city, and receive David's throne. Well, what of this David? In the Old Testament, David was called a man after the Lord's own heart. He was Israel's mightiest king. It was he who in power and glory freed Israel from political and spiritual bondage, united her tribes, and gave it the greatest prosperity and freedom that it ever enjoyed.

Just think about this for a moment. He whose birth brought a moment of peace will return again to this earth to bring a millennium of peace.

I close with this: the wise men from the east followed a comparatively small light from a star, and they found Him. Now today, if we follow that small, gentle light from within, the light of the Holy Spirit, we will find Him, who is the light and the life of the world, even the Son of God.

Chapter Thirty-Eight

Mary

From all of our Father's daughters, Mary, the mother of the Savior, was chosen to be the mother of God's almighty Son.

Mary was the noblest and greatest of all of our Father's daughters (Luke 1:28). She was of the tribe of Judah, and through her blood, the scepter of leadership would pass to Shiloh. The Lord's mother was of the royal line of King David, thus making her a princess (Luke 1:27).

Her name, Mary, is the Greek form of the Hebrew name Miriam, which means exalted (Bible Dictionary; Miriam). In a land ripe with apostasy and corruption, she was clean and pure, and worthy before the Lord.

By her obedience, she attained a place of special favor with God. He loved her, and He counted Mary as precious. Even the mighty Gabriel said, "Hail thou that art highly favored, the Lord is with thee: blessed art thou among women" (Luke 1:28).

Mary was a beautiful woman. But, what of her being a virgin? Jesus was born of a woman that there could never be even the slightest doubt or disputation whose son He was. With Gabriel's call, Mary responded, "…Behold the handmaid of the Lord; be it unto me according to thy word…" (Luke 1:38).

For all that Mary was great, Mary was humble, and I further believe that by that declaration, never was so much accepted by any woman in so few words. Even though Mary was young, she was not naïve nor uninformed. There was a maturity about her. Consider these words: "…my spirit hath rejoiced in God my Saviour" (Luke 1:47), which she said when she met Elizabeth. Mary understood the prophecies, and she had a relationship with God even before she bore His Son.

I find it inspiring that when Mary was with child, and it came to a choice between standing in public favor with Joseph as her husband or standing alone as the mother of God's Son, facing the possibility of public shame and even punishment, she chose the lonelier course. She was a woman who was true at all times. Moreover, she bore the ordeal of the journey to Bethlehem, and giving birth in the manger—and there is not the least inference in the revelations anywhere that Mary ever murmured, doubted, or wavered.

While others announced far and wide the birth of her chosen son, I find it interesting that Mary kept a disciplined and sacred silence. Mary saw and understood many things which she did not share. Through her son, the law of Moses would be fulfilled. Yet, Mary complied with that law's every command after His birth.

She was a woman of courage and determination. You'll remember that Simeon proclaimed in the Temple, "Yea, a sword shall pierce through thy own soul also…" (Luke 2:35). Mary was as close to Jesus as any human being could be. What mother does not suffer at the suffering of her babes? All that ever came upon Him, even to the spear that pierced Him at the end, came in some measure upon her. Yet, she bore it valiantly to the very end.

Mary was loyal and devoted to Joseph. Even though she was the woman chosen, and the woman of great favor, she obeyed Joseph's dreams and followed Him into Egypt, and later into Nazareth.

Similarly, she had absolute faith in her son. When she needed a miracle of wine, she came to Him. How it must have distressed her when her other sons, James, Joses, Simon and

Judah, did not understand their older brother Jesus for who and what He was (Matthew 13:55-57). Her loyalty to her son was total. In His infancy, she would protect Him; in His manhood, He would watch over her; in His Godhood, He would exalt her. All generations, now and forever, deservedly call her blessed among women.

Thank God for Mary. There is so much more about that holy woman that we do not know and cannot say, that will someday be revealed to the faithful as one of the greatest women ever to live.

Grace to Grace

Reluctantly, we must let the Christmas holiday go, but don't let that Spirit go. Do as Jesus did after His first Christmas.

When it was safe, Joseph brought Mary and Jesus out of Egypt and settled them in Nazareth of Galilee. Christmas was over and the mortal probation of God's Son was underway.

Mortality is indeed a probation. Each of us was given a body, mind, and heart, and the time, means, and a commandment to improve all three. With these gifts, we live life to love God and our fellow men. It was the same for Jesus and more so. Will the progress be slow? Will it take time and patience? Jesus waited thirty years before He was ready.

Undoubtedly, Jesus learned much from Joseph the carpenter. Luke 2:52 says that Jesus grew in "stature." He not only grew physically, but he waxed strong. There is indescribable joy in mastering and strengthening the body.

Jesus also grew spiritually. Luke says he "...waxed strong in Spirit...and the grace of God was upon Him" (Luke 2:40), and that he "increased in... favor with God..." (Luke 2:52). Jesus was close to His Father. As we study, obey, and pray, so will it be with us, and it will feel so good.

Luke also says Jesus "...increased in wisdom..." (Luke 2:52). Wisdom is vision and power. The Savior developed His mind to an astonishing degree, becoming wiser than any man in His generation, even Solomon himself. It is for us as it was for Him, we must pray and study.

It is fascinating to know that even in His youth, Jesus "increased… in favor with God and man" (Luke 2:52). He was so far above every man in every way, yet, as He increased in favor with God, He also increased in favor with man. People liked Him. In stark contrast to the hate and crucifixion at the end of His life, at the beginning, He was loved and favored by those who knew Him. He loved and was loved, as I hope happens with us.

Do as Jesus did after His first Christmas. Grow in mind, body, and spirit. Open your heart and love God and man. As we let Him in, He takes us from grace to grace, higher and higher in power and perfection of mind, body, and heart until that perfect day.

GLENN RAWSON

Glenn Rawson has been telling stories for over 30 years. He started writing as a way to share his thoughts with family and a few close friends. An acquaintance who worked in radio asked him to record and share his stories with his audience. Listeners enjoyed hearing them, and the recordings quickly spread to dozens of other stations throughout the country.

Glenn has authored more than 20 books and written and produced over 100 TV documentaries. Over the years, he has connected with millions of people through print, radio and TV broadcasts, and online social media channels.

Glenn loves to research and write, but is happiest when he is traveling the world as a tour guide, sharing stories of history and the communities he visits with his guests. His goal is to help inspire and lift others with his stories.

FOR INFORMATION ABOUT RECEIVING WEEKLY STORIES AND OTHER BOOKS AVAILABLE, PLEASE VISIT GLENNRAWSONSTORIES.COM OR HISTORYOFTHESAINTS.ORG.

FREE WEEKLY STORIES DELIVERED TO YOUR INBOX

SUBSCRIBE AT

GLENNRAWSONSTORIES.COM

JEAN TONIOLI

Jean worked as an educator for more than 30 years, and even in retirement works as adjunct faculty at Weber State University to mentor student teachers. She has always had an affinity for finding, researching, and sharing stories about her ancestors, helping to ensure their memory carries on with her family. She has four children and nine grandchildren.

Jean has a special love for piano and choir music. Her children can all recount stories of how their mother would sit at the piano bench to ensure each child would learn to play the piano. Her encouragement paid off when her son Jason started writing and arranging music.

Her talents for researching, writing, and editing have been invaluable for this book.

JASON TONIOLI

Jason is best known for his piano hymn arrangements. His career started in banking and marketing, and then he founded a successful software and consulting company. Throughout that time, he wrote several piano books and recorded and released multiple piano albums.

After the sale of his company in 2018, he was able to spend more time on his music and as of 2022 has released 15 piano solo books and 13 recorded albums. His music has been played well over 100 million times.

 He lives in Utah with his wife and four children and spends as much time being a dad as possible.